BLACK ≠ INFERIOR

Tolu' A. Akinyemi

First published in Great Britain as a softback original in 2021

Edited by The Roaring Writer Ng.

Cover Design by
Buzz Designs

Published by 'The Roaring Lion Newcastle'
ISBN: 978-1-913636-06-7

Email:
tolu@toluakinyemi.com
author@tolutoludo.com

Website:
www.toluakinyemi.com
www.tolutoludo.com

ALSO, BY Tolu' A. Akinyemi from
'The Roaring Lion Newcastle'

"Dead Lions Don't Roar" (A collection of Poetic
Wisdom for the Discerning Series 1)

"Unravel your Hidden Gems" (A collection
of Inspirational and Motivational Essays)

"Dead Dogs Don't Bark" (A collection of Poetic
Wisdom for the Discerning Series 2)

"Dead Cats Don't Meow" (A collection of Poetic
Wisdom for the Discerning Series 3)

"Never Play Games with the Devil" (A collection of
Poems)

"A Booktiful Love" (A collection of Poems)

"Inferno of Silence" (A collection of Short Stories)

Dedication

To Black People living and dead: always remember that
"Black is not a Synonym for Inferior."
We are "BLACK and UNIQUE."

TABLE OF CONTENTS

Acknowledgements 1
Poems 2

One 3

Black and Unique..4
Black Picture 5
Black Voices 6
Black Excellence I 7
Black Excellence II 8
Black Lives Matter..9
Black Boy: Hollow Vibes 10
The Police is your Friend..11
Poster Boy 12
An Aberration 13
Black Sheep 14
Black ≠ Inferior..15
Black Out 16
African Giant 17
African Time I 18
African Time II 19
Africa Arise..20
The Storm in a Glass of Water...21
Two Ticks Short..22
Black and Beautiful...23

Black as a Portrait of Criminality 24
Black Devil 25
Statues Poo 26
Black Girl: Stinking Hair 27
Sadness 28
Not Another Elegy 29
Black Unity I 30
Black Unity II 31
Nigerian Lives Matter 32
Black is Not a Synonym for Inferior 34

Two **35**

Creative Voices 36
Consensual: Not a Taboo 37
Emotional Captivity 38
Sojourners 39
Ella 40
Through the Turbulence 41
Survivors 42
Colourful Neighbour 43
Ye Are gods 44

Bio **45**
Author's Note **47**
Dead Lions Don't Roar **48**
Dead Cats Don't Meow **50**
Unravel Your Hidden Gems **52**
Dead Dogs Don't Bark **54**
Never Play Games With The Devil **56**
A Booktiful Love **58**
Inferno of Silence **60**

Acknowledgements

This is poetic—writing another book is a dream come true, for me. Sincere appreciation to God Almighty for the overflowing grace and oil that never runs dry. I'm super-grateful.

To my booktiful and loving family, Olabisi, Isaac and Abigail, thanks for the constant support on my literary journey. There is nothing like having a "home" in the literal sense to articulate my ideas.

To my parents, Gabriel and Temidayo Akinyemi, your support on this booktiful journey is deeply appreciated. And my siblings, Olushola, Oluseyi and IretiOluwa. I hold you all very dear to my heart.

A final thanks to everyone who has supported me on this journey that keeps unravelling so many booktiful experiences.

A big thank you to the editors of the journals and literary outlets below, for giving my poems their first abode.

'Survivors' first appeared in Lion and Lilac.
'Ella' first appeared in www.toluakinyemi.com

'Black and Unique' first appeared in GN Books.
'Through the Turbulence' first appeared on The Tahira Rehman Podcast Show.

POEMS

ONE

Black and Unique

I wish this can be your favourite poem;
these words, ordinances, and creed—
 a sterling light.
I wish you can see the uniqueness of your black skin,
its glory shining like a dark armour.

I wish you can rise above the tides of hate
and the contraptions of oppression.
I wish you can see, through the dawning of each day,
that you're black and unique.

I wish you can rise through the squalor of poverty
and voices that watercolour you as under-represented.
I wish you can emblaze your name in gold,
and swim against every wave of hate.

I wish you can rise above the labels—
false identities stamped on you.
You're black and unique—
I wish this can be your favourite verse.

Black Picture

This Black picture is hope to the despairing.
This Black picture is not a symbol of oppression.
It's a portraiture carved from ancient creative force.
This black picture wears grit—
a resurrection of dead dreams.

Don't paint me with the oil of perfection.
Beneath my imperfections lie the strength of a lion.
This Black picture is not a hyperbole,
it's not a concoction of a waning memory.

Black Voices

These black voices cannot be silenced.
This chorus, anthem, and movement rattle the White House.
These black voices are not a monotone.
These cries come from the pang of racism.
Today, they chorused "Black Lives Matter"
to appease the gods of vengeance.

They took a seat on the moving train
and immersed it with more than two pints of dross
before they unconsciously drifted back
to the status quo.

Black Excellence I

Black Excellence would have been an anthem
but it was lost between a grey matter
that had the colours of danger.

Before the peak of his years, his sun rose from the east
and his candle burnt brightly
on a mountain top.

He thought they would raise a glass for black excellence,
but beneath their bubbling smiles was intense scheming
to bring his moving train to a screeching halt.

Black Excellence was a cliché. His untainted legacy
was ripped to shreds by the raging mob
and enemies who don the mask of friends

chanting *jungle justice*.
He could have held the banner aloft with the inscription
Black Excellence,
but their dark hearts killed his burning light.

Black Excellence II

Black was the Genesis before there was a ray of light.
Beyonce sang *Black is King*.
I asked, "What is kingship?"
Blacks are greater than kings.

They are the fiefdom, small gods, rising ocean and standing twice as tall,
(Rocnation).
Give me one Black Mamba and the Greatest Ali,
and my walls will read **Black Excellence.**
Black is not mythical;
it is the skin gods are housed in.

Black Lives Matter

Black Lives Matter!
Don't counter this with *All lives matter!*
For if *Black Lives Matter*, then *All Lives Will Matter.*

Black Lives Matter isn't a mantra for your lying lips.
Your actions speak louder than
your sugar-coated words.

Black Lives Matter is not a drunken anthem
for the resistance army who trends *All Lives Matter*
to spite *Black Lives Matter.*

Black Lives Matter isn't a joking matter.
It isn't a wordplay for your parody accounts
and the malfeasance of that bots infested bird app.

Black Boy: Hollow Vibes

On Peckham's streets
gangsterism holds sway.
Brixton is a time-bomb.

Drugs and crime are the subterfuge
of the powers that be.
The immigrants have built a home
in our beloved Lewisham. Let's cry foul
before their imprudent ideologies run riot in our once-virgin
land.

In Harlem,
Black Boys suffer miscarriages of justice
before they become just numbers in prisons.

The Police is your Friend

Police brutality parades in matching colours of pain and
anguish.
They say the police is your friend,
but the unending hashtags—
the aftermath of police brutality—
sing a familiar tune, sorrow.
A two-headed snake with piercing stings
has the subterfuge identity of a poisoned chalice.

How do you symbolise the police without subtlety?
Drown in the pool of FEAR—
fear of not becoming a memory in people's hearts,
an unripe yam uprooted from earth.

Poster Boy

Don't adorn me with the shenanigans of diversity
in this game of unequal halves.
Throw the tag of Poster Boy far into the wild.

Your culture and norms speak volumes;
my ears are aching from the relentless bellowing
of unequal opportunities.
Don't turn my volume down—
this Black Boy won't be your poster boy.

Don't robe this black queen as your poster girl for
diversity's lead
when your actions are more brutal than a viper's bite.
When you see my yeast rising, run far to the east.
I won't be the poster boy for your false solidarity!

An Aberration

The symbols // monuments // statues // history—
slavery was a malady!
What is the difference between slave owners and human traffickers?
Some are mementoes on our streets
while the others rot behind dingy walls.

Black Sheep

Don't clothe an entire race with the toga of fraudster
because of a few bad eggs.
The fast lane, Fast cars, and Fast Life are an anathema
to the culture ingrained in us by our fathers.

Let's educate the *West* about their prejudice.
I heard three black sheep say: *we are repatriating our
colonial loot.*
Our forefathers sweat, blood and toil, which
they looted.

What loot? What repatriation?
Ambassadors of trickery.
The Gucci Master, the faux real estate mogul
who sowed tears and death,
lost the best of his years on the altar of deception.

Don't paint us black because of a few rotten apples.
Remove the weighty tag on our shoulders.
This weight of prejudice is depressing.
A thousand Black Sheep are not the archetype for an entire
race.

Black ≠ Inferior.

My shoulder pad was inflated like Burna Boy's ego
when Coachella saw the glory of the African Giant.
Ink his name in **LARGE PRINTS**—
our larger-than-life African Giant.

The one the gods of arrogance use as a specimen
when he is high and light as wind.
I will sing a song of remembrance to my young ones
to stand taller when the rails are off

and swim against the tides of racial injustice without
blinking.
My black skin is not conflicted.
It doesn't war against itself in confusion.
It's a sanctuary. A temple. A holy ground.

I won't be another statistic of your victimhood on National
Television.
I'm the truth bearer without an altar.
Black does not equate to inferior.
Black is not a synonym for an inferiority complex.

Black Out

Black gangs with Black Guns blazing.
Black Boys have been emblazoned with criminality.

My heart sinks in my chest like the Titanic underwater.
The radio says: *Another Black boy gone,*
stabbed to death by yet another Black boy.

My mouth is too heavy to sing yet another dirge
for a yam dug out in its bud. He could have been me;
could have been another Nelson Mandela, the light bearer
who liberated his people from the chains of apartheid.
He could have been a great inventor,
or the best football player of all time
(*Christ have Messi!*)

He could have been the one who walked on the moon
and caressed the galaxies. He could have been an apostle of
peace
who tied the fragments of this broken world into one piece.
He could have been anything and everything
that screamed: *I RULED MY WORLD.*
I wanted to say *Black Lives Matter.*
I have a thousand words to say.
Every time a black boy blacks out another,
my heart becomes blank, and I can feel my bones breaking.

African Giant

If this was my last album,
I would blast the music loud before I withered into
oblivion.
If this was my last book, I would litter it with big words
like a Chris Okotie sermon on a Sunday morning.

An easy way to be an African giant:
Paint dreams. Show what's Possible. Build structures.
Evolve. Grow. Die to self.

Live before leaving vivid imagery on the sands of time.
How do you eulogise a literary giant?
You celebrate this egghead
with *booktiful* words.

African Time I

The Insignia of African time etched on my skin
has no expiry date.
They said Africans are lax
and punctuality has been knocked off their consciousness...
This was seen as a fatal blow, with marks vivid, like tribal
marks.

The ghost of African time has built a dump site
in the functional part of my memory.
These words have become a recurring tune: take your time,
until the clock's chime loses its essence.

This label of African time is timeless.
There are days I try to wash it away by being the first to
arrive at banquets, but it seems It can't be wished away,
as it's an "African thing" to observe "African time."

African Time II

They said African Time is killing Africa.
But Africans have endured more killings than time can
count.
The demons confronting Africa robed in African time
are generational. Don't say 'generational curse.'

The triviality embedded in African time stinks like a sewer
On days that I could have been a stickler for timeliness.
The weight of African time on my shoulders
made me a victim for yet another time.

Africa Arise

Africa's harvest is ripe,
but it is stolen by western bandits.
Our insatiable appetite for aid soils our land.

Africa's soaring wings have been clipped
by corruption
and the prejudiced label of the West.

Africa's rising son,
whose voice echoed liberation from the apron of the West,
has been watermarked with a colossal case of corruption.

Africa's shining sun
has been darkened by a multitude of forces.
A United African front gives the West panic attacks.

But,
the African dream will not crash like a plane
from high altitudes.
Mother Africa will rise from the rubble and ashes!

Africans, burn the bridges of neo-colonialism and
imperialism!
The African time is now!

The Storm in a Glass of Water

How do you weather the storm of racism?
Turning a blind eye might leave you blinded.
Don't take sides, as this might leave you blindsided.

Calm the storm without breaking the glass
with overflowing prejudice,
as this might leave you derided, blinded, and blindsided.

Two Ticks Short

Empathy lays short, like desperate drivers
on the hunt for fuel in a scarcity season,
the clocks ticking backwards
with the world two ticks from being consumed in the
inferno.

The wind of toxicity blows with intense fury.
This conflagration of hatred cooking in the White House
is so tasteless, like undone rice.

The fabrics of humanity—tenderness,
love, and patience—no longer hold sway.
They laid the wreaths of compassion in the community
graveyard.

Black and Beautiful

Let me remind you for the umpteenth time
that Black is beautiful.
They said she was Black and ugly,
Black and Dirty,
and her Blackness was stained by false labels
that sunk her confidence.

The first television set we ever watched was in Black and
White
and it painted a vivid imagery that Black and White
are beautiful, when in Unity. They said she was Black and
Burnt
and maligned her with vile words
until she was trapped under the weight of false allusions.

Glorify your shade of Black.
Revel in its beauty.
Don't you forget
that you're Black and Beautiful.

Black as a Portrait of Criminality

This racial profiling is like a bad dream.
Blacks are the only villain in this all-cast horror movie.
This bad song on auto replay leaves a strange echo.

They profiled and profiled.
Framed and framed.
Railed and jailed.
Till my black skin became the portrait of criminality.

Black Devil

This black devil riles me like the taste of burnt *dodo* in my
tasty *Jollof.*
Hell is a fiery place with a black overlord
unleashing his fury
to sow evil in a world filled with self-righteous people.

My black shirts were burnt offerings to the gods,
the trademarks of a bad child.
Black is evil. Black is the devil. No wonder my black skin
is a trigger for overzealous white cops.

I'm looking for a soap
that can wash my blackness away
so I can be spotless like a "white angel"—
the type Hollywood has fed into our hearts as the symbol of
holiness.

Statues Poo

How do these paymasters sustain the legacy of a slave master?
Give him a statue as a legacy, with two hands in the air, screaming *I don't give two f**ks.*

How do you rewrite history?
Canonize a devil so clean, he becomes a saint
and his statue, so gallant, is a remembrance to smother the truth.

How do you discredit Black Lives Matter?
Dance naked in the marketplace with placards scribbled, "All lives matter"
but Black lives don't count.

Black Girl: Stinking Hair

How do I write a sad poem for the three-year-old girl with
the stinking hair?
Her hair's scent makes her white friends want to puke.
Prejudice and discrimination find home in innocent
classrooms.

How do I erase the teacher's voice, laminated
in the innermost parts of her heart
and her mind etched with hurting imagery of social
distancing friends?

Just write a poem about the Black girl
with the stinking hair.
Show her the glory of her hair
and the beauty of her skin
hoping that through these pages
she finds her healing.

Sadness

Can you hear my sad notes?
The pain in my voice?
Can you see the tears streaming down
the hill of my cheeks
from your prejudiced labels?
Can you see the beauty of my black skin
through your hate-tainted eyes?

Not Another Elegy

Holiness took cover when rapists desecrated the Sanctuary
in Ikpoba Hill. No one deserves to be raped, or
more-so, raped to their death.

Before the cocks crowed, the blood of another girl-child
stained a street in Ibadan. My pen bleeds and my hands
are numb from writing another elegy.

In southern Kaduna, untimely death is a constant visitor.
It's a game of death, Tears and Fear, its accomplices.
They say *the police are your friends*. We scream,

police is a synonym for untimely death.
I.   CAN'T. BREATHE.
To the white supremacists, the vibration of our soul stings
theirs with our mantra *"Black Lives Matter."*

Equality is a forgotten child. The blood of the innocents
soil the World. Racial Injustice walks tall.
The graves of our ancestors quake in anguish
at this perpetual ignominy.

Black Unity I

Black Unity is a mirage; an imaginary permutation.
Black brotherhood was buried in the backyard
for a bag of rice and five liters of oil—
that's dinner served.

Black unity died on the altar of envy
and a culture of hatred.
Where's the United front to win this raging war?
Harmony walked away from the room through the back
door,

breaking the table of their nascent brotherhood.
He said there was trinity and a united front,
but the bitterness in his heart
subversed their quest to promote Black Unity.

Black Unity II

Black Unity can't be a hoax fizzling away
like COVID-19 in Trump's brain.
The man on the high rise rose to legendary heights
with a mantra: One Black Nation.

Since his ascendancy to elevated heights, he had given
more than one Black Eye, and one black nation
was only remembered as a doormat
in his selfish quest for Black Unity.

Nigerian Lives Matter

Before you bathe me with the soap of hypocrisy
and judge me through the prism of ethnicity,
here's the closure, yet another hashtag:
#NigerianLivesMatter

Our mouths are hung to dry without sputum
as we are without strength
from our relentless quest for justice from police brutality.
#EndSars

Even those without any iota of humanity would shed tears
for the bloodbath in Southern Kaduna.
Don't read this from your tribalistic infested world-view.
#EndTerrorism

I'm out of breath by the number of times I have read the
news headline: **Boko Haram defeated**.
An unending war with unlimited war-chest
means an unending inferno with revolting battalions.
#EndthewealthbuildingmachineBokoHaram

Corruption has killed more souls than my fingers can count.
This is a war, a ravaging war triggered by humanity against
humanity.
Where is the love?
#EndCorruption

I learnt to say UP NEPA before I knew the name of my first
school.
God said *Let there be light.* Man's darkened heart
means unending blackout is our perpetual lot.
#Endblackout

The menace of *Almajiri* and Fulani herdsmen is an omen
that this matrimony will someday come to an ill-fated end
like a plane without an engine. I'm not a prophet of doom.
The skies
wear the colour of gloom stained by kisses of tribalism and
nepotism.
#Endthisunholyunion

Black is Not a Synonym for Inferior

Melanins are not inferior.
Black boy! Black girl!
Rip off that depressing garment of inferiority!

Create your mantra:
I'm not inferior!
Black is not a synonym for inferiority.

This black skin is a symbol of originality;
melanin, a shade of strength and virtues.

In their big houses, where dignity lays short,
Blacks lie on king-size beds because their rule books
scream that Black is another word for Gangsterism.

Black Child. Abused Child.
Black Child. Deprived Child.
Let this be your mantra: *I'm not inferior.*

TWO

Creative Voices

It takes years of grind and sweat to build a legacy,
untainted.
But the implosion of this *woke* generation
tethers on the realm of false allusions.

I have one thousand and one things to say
but the raging mob with sticks at my doorstep
makes my larynx crackle into folds.
My voice is imprisoned in the *woke* courts of popular
opinion

How do you string these words without being
controversial?
Submerge your creative voice in the ocean of popular
demand
and kill your conscience with political correctness.
I wanted to tell creatives
that their voice is the hope of the hopeless

I wanted to tell them to colour the sky
with their truth, but every time, my mind wanders to the
raging mob
I shed a tear for the death of truth and free speech.

Consensual: Not a Taboo

Can we end this malady
where consent is a strange word
even on desks of revered newsrooms?

Raising a girl child overwhelms me with a feeling of
melancholy
with the unrestrained hands and roving eyes of untrained
boys
doing damage.
Mother's words were episcopal:
Are your legs now being parted like an ocean?
That dress is an invitation for unforeseen evil.
Avoid night outs so you won't be an easy toast
in those dingy places where evil lurks.

In Benin, a bright candle was snuffed out, and In Ibadan,
the hijab could not save another girl from the trap of
untimely death.
My fingers hurt from typing another hashtag
#justiceforyetanothergirlchild
and my eyes are sore from seeing another rape broadcast.
 How do you resolve this malady?
Engrave Consent in the soul of every teenage boy
before they become a walking time bomb.

Emotional Captivity

Every feather to your cap leads to emotional insecurities.
The days you were on the cliff, caressing abject poverty,
love tasted sweet, without the perils of death.

Every medal in your cabinet made you a prisoner of
emotions.
This was a tug of war, not love or hate.

He echoed that they were friends for life, but every giant
stride
meant the little flame of love that held them bound
was extinguished in the dark alleys of their hearts.

He became a prisoner of flailing passions
and their nested swansong of failure resented him like a
plague.

The currency of knowledge never expires.
The currency of hate is a death-knell to every blooming
love.
He was a prisoner of emotions when his life gained turbo
speed
Like a car in full motion.

Sojourners

A novel virus was all it took for superpowers to
Drink from the same cup as the Third World and lose their
way
with abandon. The wind of sorrow
unleashes its gust each passing day.

This body, this spirit, survived the fangs of death.
The great plague swallowed all in sight.
Call us candles, burning bright today
before our lights fade and we become memories

in the hearts of lovers. Life is fickle. Tick tock,
our time is ticking. I died more times than I can remember
in the hands of fear.
We're sojourners, and it only took a novel
Virus to resonate this forgotten truth.
The great plague swallowed the mighty

and heckled at their doorposts till their walls
caved to the spirit of death. Men of little means
were not immune to its pangs...
The great plague is a
reminder that we are all sojourners in this futile world.

Ella

If Ella is a song, I will dance to the beats till I'm breathless.
Ella was the word that was spoken to heal broken hearts.
I heard these words echo: Heal-er.

If Ella was a poem,
I would read till the pages grow dog ears.
If Ella was a deity, I would worship at her temple all year
long.
How do you draw the portrait of a goddess?
That would be some *Ellawork*.

Through the Turbulence

Though the wind of sorrows blow,
and we are crushed under the weight of despair,
the agony of this plague crushing our spirits,
our faith in God is as strong as Gibraltar.

Some say there is no God because
a plague ravished the earth and
hope is gloom.
I hear them curse God,
for He seems far in the hour of need.

Last night I went to bed with a song of hope.
Today, no matter the storm that rages
and the gloom that threatens to swallow me:
I will hope on my God,
my strength and help in time of need.

God does not come late for those who trust in him.
Call us a people of faith.

Survivors

Think human bodies on sinking boats with no life jackets,
Dreams swept away by the ocean waves.
Our lives were at the mercy of rescue ships with drunken
sailors,
Our voices echoed sorrow like spring blizzards.

Their tepid hearts beat faster
than their staggering legs could carry them;
their dreams fizzled when words came from Rome:

Don't dock and dump those outcasts here.
Like rabid dogs
we found solace in concentration camps.

Then words came from Valencia
which erased the dark lines on our wrinkled faces,
immersed with a kindness note.
Bring them home.

Colourful Neighbour

My once-colourful neighbour is now a fallen tree.
I heard his mother say, *God has deserted us.*

Her once-bright smile is now a trepid frown at the
peril of an unknown future.
They said they were sons of God, but how can I tell?
God has so many Sons who do not plot evil on a graph

before they can have their name at the top of the chart.
 My once-colourful neighbour is now a forgotten
Child. His remembrance song was written with fury
and a joyful heart and immense joy.

My once-colourful neighbour is now a flickering memory.
He came in a bubble and disappeared like a
flashing light.
He departed without a wave and his bubbling smile.
We were told he was swallowed whole by a nemesis.

Ye Are gods

Don't cloak me in the garment of obscurity.
I'm a raging voice,
harbinger of the truth you loathe.

I'm from a generation of wordsmiths,
men who stir hearts with words.

I'm not just a poet, I'm a god with a GODFATHER
who anointed my head with overflowing oil
and blessed my hand with the pen of a skillful writer.

Let my epitaph bear the words:
He Lives On.
Do not cry for me, for though I may be gone,
my words make me immortal.
I'm a god; gods don't die!

He Lives On
at the tombstone of the god
whose words made him immortal.

Bio

Tolu' Akinyemi is an exceptional talent and out-of-the-box creative thinker; a change management agent and a leader par excellence. Tolu' is a business analyst, financial crime consultant, and a Certified Anti-Money Laundering Specialist (CAMS) with extensive experience working with leading investment banks and consultancy firms. Tolu' is also a personal development and career coach and a prolific writer with more than 10 years writing experience. He is a mentor to hundreds of young people. He worked as an Associate Mentor in St. Mary's School, Cheshunt and as an Inclusion Mentor in Barnwell School, Stevenage in the United Kingdom, helping students raise their aspirations and standards of performance and helping them cope with transitions from one educational stage to another.

A man whom many refer to as "Mr Vision," he is a trained economist from Ekiti State University (formerly known as University of Ado-Ekiti (UNAD)). He sat his Masters' Degree in Accounting and Financial Management at the University of Hertfordshire, Hatfield, United Kingdom. Tolu' was a student ambassador at the University of Hertfordshire, Hatfield, representing the University in major forums and engaging with young people during various assignments.

Tolu' Akinyemi is a home-grown talent; an alumnus of the Daystar Leadership Academy (DLA). He is passionate about people and wealth creation. He believes intensely that life is about impacting others. In his words, "To have a secure future, we must be willing to pay the price in order to earn the prize."

Tolu' has headlined, and been featured in, various Poetry Festivals, Open Slam, Poetry Slam, Spoken Word and Open Mic events in and outside the United Kingdom. He also inspires large audiences through spoken word performances. He has appeared as a keynote speaker in major forums and events, and facilitates creative writing master classes to many audiences.

Tolu' Akinyemi was born in Ado-Ekiti, Nigeria and lives in the United Kingdom. Tolu' is an ardent supporter of the Chelsea Football Club in London.

You can connect with Tolu' on his various Social Media Accounts:

Instagram: @ToluToludo
Facebook: facebook.com/toluaakinyemi
Twitter: @ToluAkinyemi

Author's Note

Thank you for the time you have taken to read this book. I hope you enjoyed the poems in it.

If you loved the book and have a minute to spare, I would appreciate a short review on the page or site where you bought it. I greatly appreciate your help in promoting my work. Reviews from readers like you make a huge difference in helping new readers choose the book.

Thank you!
Tolu' Akinyemi

Dead Lions Don't Roar

In a society where moral rectitude is increasingly becoming abeyant, Akinyemi's bounden duty is to reawaken it with verses. He, thus, functions as a philosopher-poet, a kind of factotum inculcating wisdom in different facets of life. Dead Lions Don't Roar leads us into the universe of an exact mind rousing the lethargic from indolence or prevarication, bearing in mind that the greatest achievers are those who take the bull by the horn. Taking a step can just be the open sesame to reach the stars. Enough of jeremiad! - **The Sun**

Dead Lions Don't Roar, a collection of poetic wisdom for the discerning, makes an interesting read. A paper pack, the poems are concise, easy to digest, travel friendly and express deep feelings and noble thoughts in beautiful and simple language. **-The Nation**

Akinyemi's verses are concise, straight-edge and explanatory, reminiscent of the kind of poetry often churned out by Mamman J. Vatsa, the late soldier and poet. **–yNaija**

Dead Lion's Don't Roar is a collection of inspiring and motivating modern-day verses. Addressing many issues close to home and also many taboo subjects, the poetry is reflective of today's struggles, and lights the way to a positive future. The uplifting book will appeal to all age groups and anyone going through change, building or enjoying a career, and facing day to day struggles. Many of the short verses will resonate with readers, leaving a sense of peace and wellbeing.

Dead Cats Don't Meow

In all, this poetry collection *Dead Cats Don't Meow* generally emphasizes the theme of self-belief and taking action. It reminds me of the saying "if you think you are too little to make an impact, try staying in a room with a mosquito." **- BellaNaija.**

Overall, *Dead Cats Don't Meow* comes across as a collection of thoughtful poetry that inspires, entertains, and educates its reader. It is a great blend of themes spanning across love, inspiration, politics, entrepreneurship, marriage and life, among others. Its simplicity eludes intentionality, and the plays on words show experience.

The collection is suitable for both the literary and non-literary community and is a great work for all manner of readers. I believe, with this one, Akinyemi has achieved his goals of motivation.

- The Nation Newspaper.

Dead Cats Don't Meow urges its readers not to waste their ninth life…the author of the collection of poetic wisdom for the discerning adds his third compendium of poems to the bookshelves alongside *Dead Lions Don't Roar* and *Dead Dogs Don't Bark*. Tolu A. Akinyemi, renowned poet, author and performer, brings to us *Dead Cats Don't Meow*, a metrical masterpiece which invokes love and respect for life with every word. Each poem examines a part of life, a sensation, a reaction, or an emotion. Beautifully written…individually, the verses breathe their own beat, whilst the collection knits together perfectly to present an idyllic collection to attain innate potential. "Don't waste the ninth life! Don't miss the chance to add this rare compendium of poetic wisdom to your bookshelf today!"

Unravel Your Hidden Gems

Unravel Your Hidden Gems is like a Solomon talking to us in the 21st century. The book teaches us to value what we have, the pursuit of excellence, and, above all, steps to unravel your hidden gems, drawn from your extraordinary talents, deposited in you right from the first day the placenta was severed from the womb. A book for all seasons, no doubt, especially in Africa where aspirations sometimes do not match inspirations, it is only logical that you add it to your shopping cart. - **Guardian Arts**

Watching others ascend the totem pole of life with relative ease, some come to believe they can't fly. Times without number, they have tried, yet they have found no way to break the ice. Don't despair if you are unsettled by a losing streak.

Tolu Akinyemi, the author of *Unravel Your Hidden Gems,* believes that the hero lies in you. If only you can discover the hidden gems in you, you are on your way to excelling. How, then, do you dig deep into the labyrinth for the gems?

Unravel Your Hidden Gems is a 376-page book by a prolific UK-based Nigerian author. It is a collection of over 360 inspirational and motivational essays from a young man who feels he has a mission to rouse dampened spirits to make the much-needed push in life to regenerate abundantly.

In seven parts, the author makes a diligent search into typical problems encountered by men, capable of weighing them down, and comes up with snippets of wisdom. **- The Sun**

Unravel your Hidden Gems is a collection of inspirational and motivational essays from the heart of the acclaimed author, Tolu' A. Akinyemi. Released hot on the heels of Tolu's first book of poetry, *Dead Lions Don't Roar*, this new book is a study on Life, encouraging people to succeed at what they feel is important to their own happiness. Be it private life, business, religion, career, or relationships, each part of life is discovered. This mind-altering life manual can be read as a whole or visited in snippets for day to day inspiration. Each essay examines and highlights challenges in life and how to succeed in enjoying life with grace. A self-help study on life with a refreshing difference, the book is a totality of life's journey, reminding us we are here on a temporary basis and that it is our duty to not hide in obscurity, but to Unravel Your Hidden Gems before it is too late! Pure Inspiration!

Dead Dogs Don't Bark

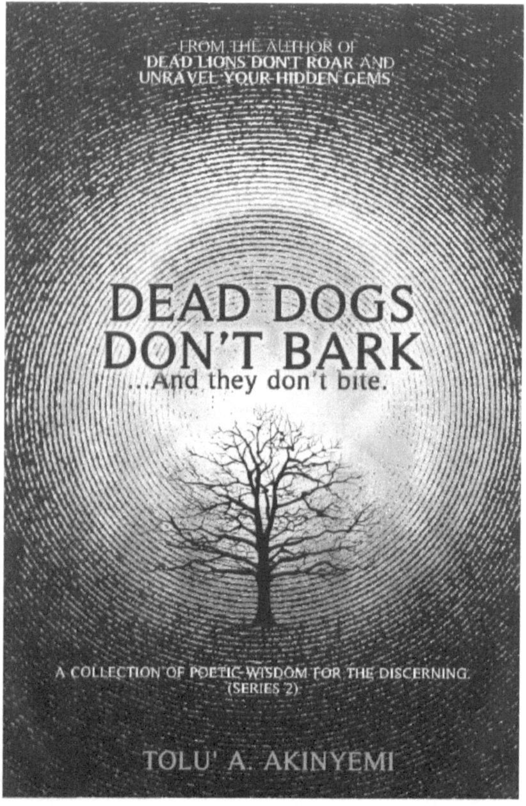

Dead Dogs Don't Bark is as culturally relevant as can be, and this deserves commendation. – **Bellanaija**

In a nutshell, Dead Dogs Don't Bark is enjoyable, it is stimulating. **- Bdaily UK**

The collection takes this reader through an exhilarating journey of wits and pun. The power of words, both grand and subtle, is that it allows the reader to place himself in the scheme and feel the poems on a more visceral level. Creating concrete imageries, the poet says even before it sticks out its tongue and bares its teeth, the first thing that defeats a fainthearted in an unfamiliar threshold is the bark of a dog. It sends cold shivers running down the spine. That very bark, disarming as it is, is the dog's way of calling attention: I am here! **- Guardian Arts**

Dead Dogs Don't Bark is the second poetry collection from the acclaimed author Tolu' A. Akinyemi. With a similar tone and style *to Dead Lions Don't Roar* (Tolu's first poetry collection) this follow-up masterpiece is nothing short of pure motivation. The poems cover a range of topics that many in life are aware of, that the Author himself has experienced and that we all, whatever our age, need support in.

Beautifully written, the poems speak volumes to all age groups as they feature finding your inner talent and celebrating your individuality and distinct voice. The poetry collection has didactic elements for evaporating the effects of peer pressure and criminality amongst many others. Also covering mental health, relationships, career focus, and general life issues, the poetry is bittersweet, amusing, and thought-provoking, in turns.

Never Play Games With The Devil

TOLU' A. AKINYEMI

Reflective, insightful, and ultimately inspirational, *Never Play Games with the Devil* is a collection best digested slowly and thoughtfully. It's a series of insights and admonitions about life's purposes and coping mechanisms for *"...not crashing under the weight of the world."*
D. Donovan, Senior Reviewer, Midwest Book Review

Readers will find Akinyemi's reflections on significant life issues completely relevant, sharply logical, and deeply felt. - **The Prairies Book Review**

Hear the poet as, in a succinct moment of self-adulation, he writes:

"My brain thinks faster than my words can convey. My mind works magic. Can I live this life forever?"

Divided into three sections, *Never Play Games with the Devil* showcases a poet at the height of his powers, exploring several themes in different voices.

In the first section, the poet is the charismatic preacher encouraging people to Hustle, Find their Feet and Grow. He writes about the lot of Broken Men crashing under the weight of expectations; he talks about boys like Eddie and Edmund, bullied for the shape of their heads. He humorously addresses the consequence of choices in the title poem, 'Never Play Games with the Devil.'

The second section secures him a seat as an activist. We see the poet tackle, in verse, despotic and undemocratic governments, marauding killer herdsmen, and the pastor who lost his voice. The poet mourns the hapless souls in the crossfire between society's rot and the State's insouciance.

The final poems explore the basis of human relationships. The poems here deal with love, commitment, and trust.

Never Play Games with the Devil is a didactic collection of poems on pertinent life issues. These poems draw their appeal from the poet's ability to sustain a figment of thought through the entire span of each poem.

A Booktiful Love

Poet Tolu' A. Akinyemi tackles life with a passionate, analytical, observing eye and creates admonitions which pull at emotional strings in the heart. Poetry readers who choose his free verse collection will find it equally powerful whether it's considering divorce and grief or the love language of 'A Booktiful Love'. - **D. Donovan - Senior Reviewer, Midwest Book Review.**

Readers will find Akinyemi's collection an intriguing approach to exploration of the entirety of human experience in its various forms. This is a superb collection. - **The Prairies Book Review.**

A Booktiful Love is a collection of poems that deal with the entirety of human experience in its various forms. Didactically rich, the poems explore ideas ranging from love, relationships, and patriotism to marriage, morality, and many other concepts pertinent to daily living.

Given its variety of themes, what unifies the poems in this collection is the simplicity and ambiguousness of language which the poet employs. The poems draw their strength from their clarity and meaning.

These are poems with a purpose. Poet Tolu' A. Akinyemi didn't shy away from this fact, as he wrote in the poems "Writers" and "Write for Rights." The poet's philosophy is evident in this collection. To him, a writer is saddled with the responsibility to use his words to teach, preach, and fight for freedom.

He writes:

"Let's change the world, one writer at a time,
Write those words till the world gets it right."

Another special attribute to this collection is the poet's experimentation with words. This is clear right from the title. The poet identifies himself as a creator of words. The reader is obliged to travel into the mind of the writer in each poem, to understand how his mind works. As readers approach the end of this collection, they not only become engrossed in its didactic richness, but also will appreciate the uniqueness of the poet's style and the sense of responsibility he carries.

Inferno of Silence

Inferno of Silence is a wide-ranging collection that tackles different themes of love, life, interpersonal relationships, and social and political challenges. It's a hard-hitting, revealing collection that keeps readers engaged and thinking with each short exploration of characters who confront their prejudices, realities, and the winds of change in their lives.

Readers of literary explorations that include African cultural influence and modern-day dilemmas will find this collection engrossing. - **D. Donovan, Senior Reviewer, Midwest Book Review**

Poignant and honest...
Akinyemi's first collection of short stories dazzles with elegant prose, genuine emotions, and Nigerian cultural lore as it plumbs both the socio-cultural issues and the depths of love, loss, grief, and personal trauma. Lovers of literary fiction will be rewarded. - **The Prairies Book Review**

The first collection of short stories by this multitalented author entwines everyday events that are articulated in excellent storytelling.

The title story "Inferno of Silence" portrays men's societal challenges and the unspoken truths and burdens that men bear, while "Black lives Matter" shows the firsthand trauma of a man facing racism as a footballer plying his trade in Europe.

Stories range from "Return Journey" where we encounter a techpreneur/ Poet/Serial Womanizer confronting consequences of his past actions, to "Blinded by Silence," where a couple united by love must face a political upheaval changing their fortune.

These are completed with stories of relationships: "Trouble in Umudike" – about family wealth and marriage; "Everybody don Kolomental" where the main character deals with mental health issues; and "In the Trap of Seers" when one's life is on auto-reverse with the death of her confidante, her mother, as she takes us through her ordeal and journey to redemption. This is a broad and very inclusive collection.

Schauen wir sie uns im Folgenden genauer an:

1.   Selbstwahrnehmung entwickeln

Wenn dir nicht bewusst geworden wäre, wie negativ sich Alkohol auf dein Leben auswirkt, würdest du jetzt nicht dieses Buch lesen. Du würdest die Tatsache, dass Alkohol die Ursache für die meisten (wenn nicht sogar alle) deiner Probleme ist, immer noch nicht erkennen und du würdest immer noch trinken. Dieser Zustand ist in der Tat gefährlich.

Deine Selbstwahrnehmung zu verbessern, ermöglicht es dir, *herauszufinden, warum* du so trinkst, wie du es tust – und das ist die Grundvoraussetzung dafür, dass du in der Lage bist, auf Alkohol zu verzichten und nüchtern zu bleiben.

Gewohnheiten entstehen aus ganz unterschiedlichen Gründen. Zu entschlüsseln, warum du tust, was du tust, erfordert eine Art von Selbstreflexion, vor der viele Menschen zurückschrecken. Allerdings lohnt es sich und bringt enorme Vorteile mit sich.

Tatsächlich treffen wir alle viele unserer Entscheidungen unbewusst – oft mit Mechanismen, die sich in der Kindheit entwickelt haben. Es ist möglich, dass frühere Ereignisse und Traumata dein Verhalten auf eine Art und Weise geprägt haben, die du gar nicht in Betracht gezogen hast.

Du hast einen Lebensstil rund um den Alkohol entwickelt und hast bestimmte Verhaltensweisen so oft wiederholt, dass sie zu einem eigenen Autopiloten geworden sind. Ehe du dich versiehst, hast du drei Drinks intus und der Kreislauf aus Trinken > Kater > Bereuen > Wiederholen beginnt von Neuem. Beim Aufbau deiner Selbstwahrnehmung geht es darum, diesen Autopiloten zu stoppen und die Kontrolle zurückzugewinnen.

Dieses Buch gibt dir die Werkzeuge, mit denen du deine Selbstwahrnehmung auf ein neues Level bringst. Du erfährst, welche Bedeutung das Unterbewusstsein und die Neuroplastizität haben und wie mächtig deine Gedanken sein können, um deine Realität zu erschaffen.

Doch zu wissen, wie du dich verändern kannst, ist nutzlos, wenn du es nicht in die Tat umsetzt.

2.   Positives Handeln

Dir vorzunehmen und zu sagen, dass du etwas tun wirst, ist einfach. Du kannst heute behaupten, dass du einen Marathon laufen, dich zum Arzt/ zur Ärztin ausbilden lassen oder das nächste durch die Decke gehende Tech-Start-up gründen wirst.

Doch die Menschen, die diese Dinge vollbringen, trainieren körperlich hart, absolvieren ein langjähriges Studium oder überstehen die Höhen, Tiefen und Rückschläge der Geschäftswelt.

Auf das Trinken zu verzichten ist nicht anders.

Es geht darum, aktiv zu werden. Nüchtern zu bleiben bedeutet, kontinuierlich zu handeln. Neben der Arbeit an deiner Selbstwahrnehmung ist es wichtig, dass du die nötigen Entscheidungen triffst und konsequent an dir arbeitest. Dazu gehört der Mut, dich selbst zu reflektieren und dir herausfordernde Fragen zu stellen, genauso wie das Selbstvertrauen, deinen eigenen Weg zu gehen – statt jeden Freitagabend mit der Meute in der Bar oder Kneipe zu enden.

Die gute Nachricht ist, dass all das mit der Zeit immer einfacher wird. Wie du gleich herausfinden wirst, ist der menschliche Geist zu tiefgreifenden Veränderungen fähig. Mit der Zeit gelingt es dir, unbewusst zu handeln und gesunde und nützliche Dinge zu tun, statt der bisherigen destruktiven Verhaltensweisen auf Autopilot.

Im Laufe der einzelnen Kapitel erfährst du, wie du deine Emotionen besser regulieren kannst und mit welchen Methoden du Auslösern, die dich zum Handeln zwingen, begegnen kannst. Diese Werkzeuge unterstützen dich dabei, auf das Trinken zu verzichten, aber auch in allen anderen Bereichen deines Lebens.

Am Ende jedes Kapitels gibt es eine kleine Aufgabe. So kannst du dich darin üben, aktiv zu werden, wobei du deine unterbewussten Überzeugungen hinterfragst und deine Selbstwahrnehmung verbesserst.

Basierend auf der Annahme, dass im Handeln eine besondere Kraft steckt, werde ich in diesem Buch immer wieder über positives Handeln sprechen. Die Dinge, die du tust, haben verschiedene Auswirkungen, und genau wie das Trinken von Alkohol und das Konsumieren von Drogen, wirkt sich nicht alles, was du tust, positiv aus!

Bedenke: Wenn das, was du tust, dich deinem Ziel nicht näher bringt – nüchtern zu bleiben und keinen Alkohol mehr zu trinken – dann ist es KEIN positives Handeln.

3.   Deine Intuition entwickeln

Sobald du an deiner Selbstwahrnehmung arbeitest und konsequent handelst, entwickelst du mit der Zeit ein feines Gespür für deine Intuition. So entsteht eine positive Wechselwirkung, bei der du unbewusst *weißt*, was du für deinen Geist, deinen Körper und deine Seele tun musst.

Du wirst lernen, wie deine Intuition der Schlüssel ist, um den negativen Kreislauf – Trinken > Kater > Gewissensbisse > Wiederholung – durch einen positiven Kreislauf zu ersetzen, der mit einem neuen Autopiloten läuft.

Sich an jedem Wochenende die Kante zu geben und an den Wochentagen immer wieder einen Kater zu haben, ist auch ein Kreislauf – aber es ist keiner, den du in deinem Leben haben möchtest. Es ist genau der Teufelskreis, der zu all dem „Nie wieder" führt.

***

Für wen ist dieses Buch gedacht?

Wenn du es ernst damit meinst, mit dem Alkohol aufzuhören und wenn du Werkzeuge nutzen möchtest, die dich dabei unterstützen, ein Leben zu führen, auf das du stolz sein kannst, dann ist dieses Buch genau das Richtige für dich.

Auch wenn du schon seit einiger Zeit nüchtern bist, kannst du die Werkzeuge in diesem Buch nutzen, um deine Widerstandsfähigkeit zu erhöhen und jeden Bereich deines Lebens zu verbessern. Am Ende dieses Buches wirst du dich wie ein nüchterner Jedi fühlen, der bereit ist, das Nüchternsein auf einem alkoholisierten Planeten zu meistern.

An dieser Stelle sollte unbedingt erwähnt werden, dass ein „kalter Entzug" von Alkohol für regelmäßige und starke Trinker aufgrund der körperlichen Entzugserscheinungen extrem gefährlich sein kann. Es kann zu Übelkeit, Schlaflosigkeit, zittrigen Händen und Kopfschmerzen kommen, aber auch lebensbedrohliche Symptome wie Krampfanfälle, Halluzinationen und Bluthochdruck hervorrufen.[2] Deshalb solltest du deinen Arzt konsultieren, bevor du einen Alkoholentzug machst, falls du auch nur den geringsten Verdacht hast, dass du körperlich abhängig sein könntest.

Im hinteren Teil dieses Buches findest du weitere Informationen über körperliche Entzugserscheinungen. Wenn du diese Informationen liest, wirst du *dich selbst besser wahrnehmen* können und in der Lage sein, *positiver zu handeln*, um deinen eigenen Bedürfnissen besser nachzukommen.

Überlasse es nicht dem Zufall – wenn du glaubst, dass du unter Entzugserscheinungen leidest, sprich jetzt mit einem Arzt oder einer Ärztin. Das ist dein Aufruf zum *Handeln*.

***

Dieses Buch ist eine Fortsetzung von *Nüchtern auf einem alkoholisierten Planeten - Ohne Alkohol leben*. Es funktioniert allerdings sowohl als Zusatzlektüre als auch als eigenständiges Buch. Das vorherige Buch bringt dich dazu, zu hinterfragen, warum Alkohol überhaupt ein so großer Teil deines Lebens ist, und bietet dir *Ansatzpunkte*, um auf Alkohol zu verzichten. Dieses Buch geht den nächsten Schritt auf diesem Weg – es gibt dir die Methoden und Werkzeuge an die Hand, um mit dem

Alkoholkonsum aufzuhören und nüchtern zu bleiben.

Die Anleitungen in diesem Buch sind das Ergebnis vieler „Aha-Momente" auf dem Weg zur Nüchternheit. Dazu gehörten der Besuch einer Reha-Klinik, Gruppentreffen der Anonymen Alkoholiker, Gruppentherapie und jede Menge Einzeltherapie. Da ich von der Persönlichkeitsentwicklung, die ich nüchtern erleben konnte, geradezu besessen war, habe ich mehr als 3000 Stunden damit verbracht, Bücher zu diesem Thema zu lesen und zu hören.

Als ausgebildeter Therapeut und Krafttrainer lasse ich mich auch von meiner beruflichen Erfahrung inspirieren, wenn ich Menschen dabei begleite, ihren Körper und ihren Geist zu stärken. Weitere wertvolle Erkenntnisse stammen aus der „Sober On A Drunk Planet"-Community und von den vielen Menschen, die ich für den „Sober On A Drunk Planet"-Podcast interviewt habe.

Ich habe viele Jahre damit verbracht, mir meiner selbst bewusst zu sein und zu wissen, dass ich mit dem Trinken aufhören *sollte*. Das „Vergnügen", das ich dabei empfand, wurde bei weitem von den Auswirkungen aufgewogen – von meinen Finanzen bis hin zu meiner körperlichen und geistigen Gesundheit. Es gibt allerdings einen deutlichen Unterschied zwischen der Erkenntnis, dass du etwas tun *solltest*, und dem tatsächlichen Tun.

Nüchternheit schafft einen positiven Kreislauf, der dein Leben verändert und dich immer wieder aufs Neue belohnt. Er ersetzt den negativen Teufelskreis von „Trinken > Freizeit vergeuden > verkatert zur Arbeit gehen > in der nächsten Woche das Ganze wiederholen, weil du das immer so gemacht hast".

Das musst du NIE wieder tun.

Bevor wir loslegen, hier eine kurze Zusammenfassung dessen, was du auf den nächsten Seiten erwarten kannst:

Im ersten Kapitel beginnen wir mit der grundlegenden Arbeit an der Selbstwahrnehmung. Zuerst schauen wir uns an, wie viel von dem, was wir tun, auf unbewussten Entscheidungen basiert und wie viele Menschen dadurch im negativen Teufelskreis von „Nie wieder" stecken bleiben.

Du weißt bereits, dass es dir nicht gut tut, wenn du Woche für Woche trinkst und dabei ein stetig wachsendes Bereuen und ein schlechtes

Selbstwertgefühl aufbaust. Wenn du das erste Kapitel liest, wirst du anfangen zu verstehen, warum du das tust – und wie du damit *aufhören* kannst.

Im zweiten Kapitel geht es darum, wie wichtig es ist, sich Ziele zu setzen. Hier lernst du, wie du dich von einer Person, die darüber spricht, was sie vorhat, zu einer Person entwickelst, die tatsächlich aktiv wird. Außerdem geht es um die Bedeutung der Intuition und warum ihre Entwicklung die „geheime Zutat" ist, um deine Nüchternheit zu meistern.

Im dritten Kapitel geht es um die emotionale Intelligenz und darum, dass regelmäßiger Alkoholkonsum sie garantiert beeinträchtigt. Hier lernst du, wie du auf gesunde Weise mit deinen Emotionen umgehen kannst, statt sie mit Alkohol zu betäuben. Dieses Kapitel ist entscheidend, um auf Dauer nüchtern zu bleiben und den großen roten „Scheiß drauf"-Knopf loszuwerden, der bei uns allen herumspukt!

Im vierten Kapitel geht es um das Verlangen und die Trigger. Hier erfährst du, wie du sie erkennen und bewältigen kannst, denn für viele Menschen ist genau das der Grund, warum es leicht war, sich gegen das Trinken zu entscheiden, aber schwer, nüchtern zu bleiben.

Wenn du verstehst, wie diese Faktoren funktionieren, und die in diesem Buch beschriebenen Methoden und Techniken erlernst, wirst du die Kraft haben, ihnen zu widerstehen.

In Kapitel fünf widmen wir uns dem Ego. Es zu verstehen, kann der Schlüssel zu lang anhaltender, erfüllender Nüchternheit sein. Hier triffst du auf „Tommy Tequila" und „Wendy, die Trinkerin" und erfährst, wie du dich vom betrunkenen Ego zu einem positiven nüchternen Ego entwickeln kannst.

Im sechsten Kapitel geht es darum, deine Nüchternheit zu stärken und sie dauerhaft zu erhalten. Es geht um den Aufbau von Resilienz und positiven Gewohnheiten.

Regelmäßiges Trinken ist eine Gewohnheit, die Beharrlichkeit und Engagement erfordert. „Das Leben auf Sparflamme leben" beschreibt, was es heißt, mit einem Kater und einem niedrigen Energielevel durchs Leben zu gehen - ganz zu schweigen von der schlechten körperlichen Gesundheit und dem überzogenen Bankkonto.!

Positive Gewohnheiten sind unendlich viel wertvoller. Dieses Kapitel unterstützt dich dabei, positive Gewohnheiten zu entwickeln, die wiederum zu gesünderen Kreisläufen führen.

In Kapitel sieben beschäftigen wir uns mit der Verbindung zwischen Körper und Geist. Trotz der vielen fragwürdigen Artikel darüber, wie ein gelegentliches Glas Wein „gut für dich" ist, ändert keiner etwas an der Tatsache, dass Alkohol ein Gift ist, das der körperlichen und geistigen Gesundheit ernsthaft schaden kann.

Um ein gesundes und erfülltes Leben ohne Alkohol zu führen, ist das Verständnis für die Bedeutung von Bewegung und Ernährung der Schlüssel. An dieser Stelle werfen wir einen Blick auf die Wissenschaft dahinter, damit du Entscheidungen treffen kannst, die dir wirklich gut tun.

Schließlich sprechen wir im achten Kapitel über Energie und ihre positiven oder negativen Schwingungen. Millionen von Menschen auf der ganzen Welt wenden Praktiken an, die sich auf den Fluss von Energie beziehen – von Akupunktur über Reiki bis hin zu Qigong.

Ob dir solche Aktivitäten gefallen oder nicht, ist (in diesem Stadium) gar nicht entscheidend. Es ist nicht nötig, ein Qigong-Meister zu sein, um verschiedene Energien um dich herum zu spüren

– die von Menschen, Umgebungen und Situationen. Die Energie, die du sonntagmorgens im Fitnessstudio spürst, ist ganz anders als die am Morgen nach einer durchzechten Nacht!

Auch hier spielt die Selbsterkenntnis eine große Rolle. Wenn du dir deiner eigenen Energie und der Energie um dich herum bewusst bist, kannst du vermeiden, dass deine Nüchternheit durch die Orte, an die du gehst, die Dinge, die du tust, und die Menschen, mit denen du Zeit verbringst, gefährdet wird.

In allen Kapiteln begegnen wir immer wieder dem zentralen Thema der *3 Nüchternen Schritte*:

Eine verbesserte **Selbstwahrnehmung**, kombiniert mit **positivem Handeln**, wird dir ermöglichen, deine **Intuition** zu verbessern. So kannst du bessere, gesündere und wertvollere Entscheidungen für dich treffen.

Wenn es dich nicht herausfordert, verändert es dich nicht – *3 Nüchterne Schritte* werden dich kontinuierlich herausfordern, mehr zu *erfahren*, mehr zu *tun* und mehr zu *fühlen*, damit du auf das Trinken verzichten und deine Nüchternheit meistern kannst.

Bist du bereit, aus dem „Nie wieder!" ein „Das machen wir wieder!" zu machen? Lass uns loslegen und mit der lohnenswerten Kunst der Selbstwahrnehmung anfangen.

KAPITEL 1:

DU WEISST NICHT, WAS DU NICHT WEISST (UND WAS DU WEISST, IST VIELLEICHT NICHT GANZ KORREKT!)

Was ist Selbstwahrnehmung?

Laut der Definition im Lexikon ist es das „Wissen und Verstehen des eigenen Charakters". [3] Im Jahr 1972 schlugen zwei Psychologen jedoch eine aufschlussreichere Beschreibung vor:

„Selbstwahrnehmung ist die Fähigkeit, sich auf sich selbst zu konzentrieren und zu erkennen, ob die eigenen Handlungen, Gedanken und Gefühle mit den eigenen Maßstäben übereinstimmen oder nicht. Wer sich selbst wahrnimmt, kann sich selbst objektiv einschätzen, die eigenen Emotionen steuern, das eigene Verhalten mit den eigenen Werten in Einklang bringen und richtig verstehen, wie andere dich wahrnehmen." [4]

Lass uns das auf den regelmäßigen Alkoholkonsum anwenden und an das verkatertes „Nie wieder"-Gefühl denken, über das wir in der Einleitung gesprochen haben.

Wenn du dein Verhalten regelmäßig bereust, entspricht es sicherlich nicht deinen Werten. Und wenn du wieder mit einem Kater aufwachst, weil du wieder mehr Alkohol getrunken hast, als du vorhattest, hat dein Verhalten ganz bestimmt nicht mit deinen inneren Werten übereingestimmt!

Die gute Nachricht ist, dass du damit bei weitem nicht allein bist. Selbstwahrnehmung ist eine Fähigkeit, die viele Menschen nur schwer entwickeln können. Denk mal an deine Freunde und deine Familie. Du kennst bestimmt die Verhaltensmuster mancher Personen, die für alle anderen offensichtlich sind, außer für sie selbst. Möglicherweise ist sogar offensichtlich, was sie ändern sollten.

Schwieriger ist es, die Linse auf sich selbst zu richten. Es lohnt sich, aber es erfordert Mut, dies zu tun. Außerdem ist es nichts, was du in der Lage zu tun bist, wenn du in einem Kreislauf aus Betrunken- und Verkatertsein feststeckst.

Wie hilft dir also mehr Selbstwahrnehmung dabei, auf das Trinken zu verzichten und nüchtern zu bleiben?

Damit du den Zusammenhang verstehst, hier ein weiteres Zitat von dem inspirierenden österreichischen Psychiater und Philosophen Viktor Frankl:

„Zwischen Reiz und Reaktion gibt es einen Raum. In diesem Raum haben wir die Freiheit und die Macht, unsere Reaktion zu wählen. In unserer Reaktion liegen unser Wachstum und unsere Freiheit." [5]

Millionen von Menschen reagieren auf alle möglichen Stimuli, indem sie Alkohol trinken. Harte Woche auf der Arbeit? Direkt in die Bar zur Happy Hour – für ein weiteres „nur ein oder zwei", das sich in eine durchzechte Nacht verwandelt. Ein Grund zum Feiern? Eine Flasche Champagner. Die Sonne ist aufgegangen? Dann trink lieber ein Bier! Dein Team hat gewonnen? Trinken wir, um zu feiern. Deine Mannschaft hat verloren? Trinken wir, weil es bedauerlich ist.

Es mag so aussehen, als würden das *alle* tun. In deinem Bekanntenkreis tun das vielleicht auch alle! Aber es sind NICHT alle. Eine Studie über die erwachsene Weltbevölkerung ergab, dass 58% der Menschen in den letzten 12 Monaten überhaupt keinen Alkohol getrunken haben.[6]

Diese Menschen bekommen auch schlechte Nachrichten. Sie haben anstrengende Arbeitstage, nehmen an Hochzeiten und Beerdigungen teil und kommen mit all den guten und schlechten Dingen zurecht, die das Leben für sie bereithält (all das müssen sie nicht verkatert tun!)

Es erscheint verrückt, dass das Trinken von Alkohol die automatische Reaktion auf so viele unterschiedliche Situationen zu sein scheint, sowohl auf gute als auch auf schlechte. Es ist verrückt, aber ganz so einfach ist es auch wieder nicht.

Wenn du nach einer langen Woche dein E-Mail-Postfach zumachst, sitzt du ja nicht bewusst da und denkst: „Was ist die beste Lösung für meine Gefühle wie Müdigkeit, Ohnmacht und Frustration?" Stattdessen treffen wir viele Entscheidungen unbewusst auf der Grundlage dessen, was die anderen um uns herum tun, wie wir konditioniert wurden und was wir glauben, dass wir damit den Tag überstehen werden.

Alkohol baut Stress ab (in einer sehr beschränkten und vorübergehenden Weise). Alkohol lässt uns „vergessen". Doch kannst du dir wirklich vorstellen, dass er die Lösung für Stress ist? Wenn du das ganze Wochenende trinkst, fühlst du dich dann weniger gestresst, wenn dir am Montagmorgen auf dem Weg zur Arbeit übel ist? Bist du stolz darauf, dass du mehr ausgegeben hast, als du wolltest, und nichts von dem gemacht hast, was du eigentlich vorhattest?

Die Sache ist die: Wir sind darauf konditioniert, Alkohol als Lösung zu sehen. Die Fernsehwerbung zeigt Menschen, die glamourös und sorglos aussehen, während sie 40 %-Spirituosen trinken. Der Morgen danach wird nie gezeigt, denn seien wir ehrlich: Du würdest nie wieder Alkohol kaufen, wenn Werbung auch die negativen Auswirkungen, die er mit sich bringt, zeigen würde! Wir sind umgeben von der „Wine o'clock"- Kultur, Bars, Restaurants und Geschäften, die Alkohol verkaufen.

Wenn dir bewusst wird, was Alkohol tatsächlich mit dir macht, im Gegensatz zu dem, was die Gesellschaft dir vorgegaukelt hat – dann fängst du an, deinen Fokus zu verändern.

Warum das, was wir glauben, nicht unbedingt wahr ist

Jahrelang habe ich getrunken und war in dem trügerischen Glauben, dass Alkohol einen positiven Einfluss auf mein Leben hat:

- Ich glaubte, dass Alkohol die einzige Möglichkeit sei, meine Freizeit zu genießen und Kontakte zu knüpfen.
- Ich glaubte, Alkohol sei ein Mittel zur Bewältigung einer stressigen Woche und ein effektiver Weg, um mit meinen Problemen fertig zu werden.
- Ich glaubte, dass Alkohol mich für das andere Geschlecht attraktiver machte.
- Ich glaubte, dass ich witziger war, wenn ich getrunken hatte, und die Leute haben mir das auch gesagt (was meinen Glauben bestätigte)!
- Ich glaubte, wenn ich keinen Alkohol trinke, bin ich weniger ein Mann.
- Ich glaubte, dass Menschen, die keinen Alkohol trinken, nicht vertraut werden kann.
- Ich glaubte, ich sei ein besserer Fahrer, wenn ich getrunken hatte (das war illegal und gefährlich!).

Diese Glaubenssätze entstanden durch eine Kombination aus dem Folgenden:

- Gesellschaftliche Konditionierung (ich lebe in London, und ja, wir Briten haben unseren Ruf als Trinker zu Recht!)
- Familiäre und kulturelle Konditionierung (ich bin halb Ire und halb Italiener - Guinness *und* Wein!)
- Ich bin mit Freunden aufgewachsen, die EXAKT dieselben Überzeugungen in Bezug auf Alkohol vertraten.

Diese Glaubenssätze in Bezug auf Alkohol wurden in der Schule, an der Universität, in der Geschäftswelt, in meinem Golf-, Fußball-, Rugby- und Kricketclubs und sogar bei dem einen Mal, als ich einen Laufclub besuchte (nie wieder!), bekräftigt. Alkohol war an diesen Orten immer ein RIESIGER Bestandteil.

Bei allen möglichen Anlässen wurden diese Glaubenssätze bekräftigt: Feiertage, Geburtstage, Beerdigungen, Hochzeiten, Scheidungsfeiern, Geschäftsessen, Festivals, Verabredungen, Ostern, Picknicks, Flusskreuzfahrten, Sternenbeobachtung, Sonnenaufgänge, Sonnenuntergänge, Weihnachten, Silvester, Neujahr... die Liste ginge endlos so weiter.

Selbst eine der beliebtesten Gruppen auf Peloton heißt #pelo4wine. Sich eine Stunde lang abzustrampeln, um sich mit einem chemischen Depressivum zu belohnen, scheint verrückt. Doch auch im Fitnessbereich gibt es Gruppen, die die Botschaft bekräftigen, dass Alkohol eine Belohnung ist!

Wir leben tatsächlich auf einem alkoholisierten Planeten.

Wenn du von Leuten umgeben bist, die alle dasselbe glauben, kommst du lange nicht auf die Idee, irgendetwas anders zu machen oder die „Norm" zu sprengen. Ein Verzicht auf Alkohol hätte zu jeder Zeit vor meiner Reha allem widersprochen, woran ich geglaubt habe!

Wie du siehst, bewirkt die Konditionierung nichts anderes, als dass du eine Reihe von Glaubenssätzen über Alkohol aufbaust. Diese werden dann von den Menschen bestätigt, mit denen du an den Orten abhängst, die du besuchst, oder sogar von der Peloton-Gruppe, der du dich anschließt!

Du hast keine Chance, dich zu ändern, solange du dich nicht für die Möglichkeit öffnest, dass **das, was du glaubst, nicht unbedingt wahr**

ist. Es ist möglicherweise ein falscher Glaubenssatz.

Mein Irrglaube, dass Alkoholkonsum mich selbstbewusster und attraktiver bei Frauen macht, stand im krassen Gegensatz zur Realität. Die meiste Zeit meiner Zwanziger war ich ein hoffnungsloser Single! Ich hatte viel mehr peinliche als romantische Erlebnisse. War mein Glaubenssatz, dass Alkohol mich attraktiver und selbstbewusster macht, richtig?

Nein. Das war er nicht!

Hier ist ein weiteres Beispiel für einen falschen Glaubenssatz:

„Das habe ich jetzt gebraucht" sind Worte, die oft von denen gesagt werden, die glauben, dass Alkohol Stress abbauen kann. Wir haben das alle schon mal gehört!

Wenn wir davon ausgehen, dass Alkohol Stress abbaut, ist es kein Wunder, dass wir nach einer stressigen Woche in die Bar gehen oder zu Hause eine Flasche Wein öffnen. Aber das Problem wird deutlich, wenn wir erkennen, dass es das Schlimmste ist, einem bereits gestressten Körper und Gehirn Alkohol zuzuführen.

In meinem letzten Buch, *Nüchtern auf einem alkoholisierten Planeten - Leben ohne Alkohol*, habe ich mich mit den wissenschaftlichen Grundlagen dieses Themas beschäftigt. Um Alkohol zu verarbeiten, schüttet der Körper Cortisol aus. Cortisol ist buchstäblich als das Stresshormon bekannt.[7] Physiologisch gesehen ist es unmöglich, dass Alkohol wirklich Stress abbaut.

Um mit diesem Paradox umzugehen, lassen wir uns auf etwas ein, das als kognitive Dissonanz bekannt ist. Das ist „der mentale Konflikt, der auftritt, wenn die Verhaltensweisen und Glaubenssätze einer Person nicht übereinstimmen".[8]

Warum wir tun, was wir tun, obwohl wir eigentlich wissen, dass wir es nicht tun sollten

Kognitive Dissonanz kann sich in allen möglichen Bereichen deines Lebens einschleichen. Nach dieser Theorie empfinden Menschen „Unbehagen und Anspannung", wenn sie „zwei Glaubenssätze vertreten, die einander widersprechen". Das ist so, als ob du fit und gesund sein willst, aber nie ins Fitnessstudio gehst. Du fühlst dich schuldig, weil du nicht ins

Fitnessstudio gehst, und ärgerst dich darüber, dass du nicht fit und gesund bist!

Um uns wohler zu fühlen und unser Unbehagen zu lindern, lassen wir uns auf verschiedene Verhaltensweisen ein. Zum Beispiel „erklären wir Dinge weg" oder „lehnen Informationen ab, die im Widerspruch zu unseren bestehenden Überzeugungen stehen".

Die Aufrechterhaltung der kognitiven Dissonanz ist eine einfachere und bequemere Option als das zu tun, was du tun *solltest* – vor allem, wenn es darum geht, Glaubenssätze in Frage zu stellen, die vielleicht seit der Kindheit verankert sind.

Beim Alkoholkonsum ist das nicht anders. Wenn du zum Beispiel jemanden sagen hörst: „Ich trinke nicht so viel wie diese und jener", dann erklärt die Person damit nur, dass das Trinken der Person selbst problematisch sein könnte. Ich persönlich habe meinen Alkohol- und Drogenkonsum früher auf alles und jeden geschoben, um mich nicht mit der Realität auseinandersetzen zu müssen.

Kognitive Dissonanz macht sich vor allem dann bemerkbar, wenn ein Arzt einem Trinker sagt, dass die empfohlene Höchstmenge sechs Biere oder sechs Gläser Wein pro Woche beträgt.[9] In diesem Momenten vergessen wir, dass wir an einem Freitagabend acht Drinks zu viel getrunken haben!

Wenn du die Risiken und Realitäten des Trinkens kennst (und es ist nicht schwer, sie zu erfahren), *musst* du dich auf kognitive Dissonanzen einlassen, um weiter zu trinken. Wenn du die Fakten kennst und erkennst, dass Alkohol keinen Stress abbaut, *brauchst* du ebenfalls kognitive Dissonanz, um dir einzureden, dass er es doch tut.

Die mentale Gymnastik, die nötig ist, um das durchzuhalten, ist anstrengend. Dennoch tun die Leute das über Jahrzehnte. Ich jedenfalls habe es getan. Manche Menschen halten das sogar ein Leben lang durch.

Es gibt verschiedene Möglichkeiten, kognitive Dissonanz aufrechtzuerhalten. Du wirst sie zweifellos erkennen – von dir selbst und den Menschen um dich herum.

Eine davon ist, „sich zu weigern, neue Informationen aufzunehmen, die (deinen) Vorstellungen widersprechen". Das bedeutet, den fragwürdigen „Rotwein ist gut für dich"-Artikeln Aufmerksamkeit zu schenken – aber die vielen anderen zu ignorieren, die von sehr realen Gesundheitsrisiken sprechen.

Das ist ein Phänomen, das als „Priming"[10] bekannt ist, bei dem dein Gehirn selektiv Informationen herausfiltert, die deinen bestehenden Glaubenssätzen – oder dem, was du glauben *möchtest* – widersprechen, damit du dein Leben weiterführen kannst, ohne herausfordernde Veränderungen vornehmen zu müssen.

Zum Beispiel: „Alkohol macht mich für Frauen attraktiv" versus „Ich sollte nüchtern werden und an meinem Selbstwertgefühl arbeiten, mit dem ich seit meiner Kindheit Probleme habe, damit ich eines Tages jemanden mit meinem natürlichen Charme anziehen kann!"

Das Gehirn ist bereits erschöpft, wenn es über die zweite Option nachdenkt, also entscheidet es sich für das, was am einfachsten ist – den nächsten Drink bitte!

Eine andere Möglichkeit, die kognitive Dissonanz aufrechtzuerhalten, besteht darin, sich selbst von der Teilnahme an Diskussionen über bestimmte Themen auszuschließen. Für Trinker ist es einfach, sich immer mit denselben

Leuten zu treffen, die regelmäßig trinken. Wenn es alle tun, fühlt es sich normal an.

Wenn sich jemand bei einer dieser Trinkergruppen als nüchtern vorstellt, wirst du hören, wie sich die Leute für ihr Trinken rechtfertigen und sagen, dass sie „nicht so oft trinken"! Trinkende haben dann das Gefühl, dass sie sich verteidigen müssen!

Der berühmte Wirtschaftswissenschaftler John Kenneth Galbraith sagte: „Vor die Wahl gestellt, entweder die eigene Meinung zu ändern oder zu beweisen, dass es keine Notwendigkeit dafür gibt, entscheiden sich fast alle für Letzteres."[11]. Das ist kognitive Dissonanz.

Die Alternative zur kognitiven Dissonanz wäre, deine Überzeugungen zu hinterfragen und gegebenenfalls zu verändern.

Das bedeutet, dass du bereit bist, dich weiterzuentwickeln – und diese Herausforderung ist anspruchsvoller, als einfach immer wieder das Gleiche zu tun. Es bedeutet, dass du dich traust, die beunruhigenden Artikel (und eventuell auch deine Kontoauszüge) zu lesen! Es bedeutet, dass du dich entscheiden solltest, welche dieser widersprüchlichen Glaubenssätze und Verhaltensweisen du für den

Rest deines Lebens wirklich leben möchtest. Und wenn du im „Nie wieder"-Kreislauf feststeckst, ist dir vielleicht schon klar, welche Glaubenssätze für dich nicht funktionieren.

Wir werden uns ansehen, wie du deine Selbstwahrnehmung verbessern und du mit diesen falschen Glaubenssätzen aufräumen kannst.

Selbstwahrnehmung und das innere Kind

Deine Glaubenssätze zu hinterfragen und zu ändern, bedeutet auch, mit deinem inneren Kind in Kontakt zu kommen und dir selbst bewusster zu werden, wie frühere Erfahrungen dich geprägt haben.

Warum ist das wichtig, um mit dem Trinken aufzuhören und nüchtern zu bleiben??

Selten sind der Alkohol oder die Drogen das eigentliche Problem. Vielmehr wird die Sucht zu einem sekundären Problem, um vergangene Ereignisse oder Traumata zu verdrängen.

Das liegt daran, dass sich viele der Denkmuster, die deine Emotionen beeinflussen (und damit auch das, was du tust), bereits lange bevor du dir dessen bewusst bist, gebildet werden. Studien haben gezeigt, dass „es signifikante Zusammenhänge zwischen unseren Verhaltenstendenzen im Alter von wenigen Monaten und unserer späteren Persönlichkeit gibt".[12]

Das bedeutet, dass du nicht als eine Person geboren wurdest, die ständig zu viel trinken wird. Es ist jedoch schwer zu bestreiten, dass unsere frühen Erfahrungen einen Einfluss darauf haben, wie wir uns selbst sehen und mit der Welt um uns herum interagieren. Mit den Worten des Wissenschaftlers Dr. Carl Sagan[13]: „Solange wir unsere Vergangenheit nicht vollständig verstehen, werden wir nie wirklich in der Gegenwart leben."

Trauma ist ein heikles Thema. Für verschiedene Menschen hat es unterschiedliche Bedeutungen. Es ist alles relativ, und es gibt keine bestimmte Grenze, ab der ein Kindheitstrauma als so schlimm angesehen wird, dass es sich auf dein Leben als Erwachsener auswirkt.

Einige Arten von Kindheitstraumata haben eindeutige Auswirkungen. Kinder, die körperlich, sexuell oder emotional missbraucht wurden, erleben beispielsweise im Erwachsenenalter eher belastende Trigger, die zu einem Missbrauch von Alkohol und anderen Substanzen führen können. Zahlreiche Studien belegen diesen Zusammenhang.[14] Aber Traumata gibt es in allen Formen und Ausprägungen.

Die meisten Menschen gehen davon aus, dass sie in ihrer Kindheit kein nennenswertes Trauma erlebt haben. Sie ziehen nicht in Betracht, dass das Gefühl, auf dem Spielplatz ausgegrenzt worden zu sein, weil sie nicht sportlich waren oder nicht die gleichen Spielsachen wie ihre Altersgenossen hatten, ein ernsthaftes Trauma für ihr inneres Kind ausgelöst haben könnte. Es ist gut möglich, dass sie dadurch Bewältigungsmechanismen entwickelt haben, die bis zum heutigen Tag bestehen.

Es gibt unendlich viele ähnliche Beispiele: im Schatten eines begabten Geschwisterkinds aufzuwachsen, ignoriert oder vernachlässigt zu werden, sich anders zu fühlen oder in einem Haushalt zu leben, der mit gesundheitlichen, finanziellen oder tausend anderen Problemen zu kämpfen hatte.

Oft findet die Reaktion auf dieses Trauma und der Zwang, es zu „begraben", im Unterbewusstsein statt. Infolgedessen erinnerst du dich vielleicht gar nicht mehr an die

Ereignisse in deiner Kindheit, die dich zu dem gemacht haben, was du heute bist.

Deshalb ist es so wichtig, sich seiner selbst bewusst zu werden und in Kontakt mit dem inneren Kind zu kommen. Es bringt dich an den Punkt, an dem du nicht nur weißt, was du tust, sondern auch, *warum du es tust.*

Sich nur auf die Lösung zu konzentrieren, d.h. mit dem Alkoholkonsum aufzuhören, ist nur ein Teil der Formel für eine starke Genesung. Indem wir vergangene Traumata in der Gegenwart bewältigen, werden wir stärker und widerstandsfähiger gegenüber den traumatischen Erlebnissen.

Wenn dich ein Ereignis triggert, kann es enorm überwältigend sein und dazu führen, dass du zur Flasche greifst, um dir vorübergehend Erleichterung zu verschaffen. Das Ereignis kann darin bestehen, dass jemand auf eine bestimmte Weise mit dir spricht oder einen Teil deines Körpers berührt, der dich in ein vergangenes Trauma zurückversetzt. All das kann unbewusst passieren, ohne dass du bewusst Kontrolle darüber hast.

Die Arbeit mit dem inneren Kind ist ein WESENTLICHER Bestandteil der Bewältigung zukünftiger Situationen. Sie wird dich dabei unterstützen, vergangene Traumata zu überwinden und zu bewältigen, damit sie dich heute nicht mehr beeinflussen.

Es IST möglich, die Kontrolle über dein Unterbewusstsein zurückzuerlangen, indem du dein Unterbewusstsein neu verschaltest (oder umprogrammierst). Wenn du dir deiner selbst bewusster wirst, kannst du die Dinge verlangsamen und verhindern, dass dieser Kreislauf auf Autopilot läuft.

Die Umstellung des Unterbewusstseins beginnt „mit der Entscheidung, was du möchtest – jetzt und in Zukunft – und der Fokussierung darauf".[15] Wenn du dieses Buch durcharbeitest, lernst du, dir selbst mehr Aufmerksamkeit zu schenken und beginnst, einige deiner unterbewussten Glaubenssätze zu verstehen und zu hinterfragen.

Selbstwahrnehmung entwickeln, um nüchtern zu bleiben und darüber hinaus

Wie wir bereits festgestellt haben, ist die Selbstwahrnehmung der Schlüssel, um uns aus alten Mustern zu befreien und gesündere

Verhaltensweisen zu entwickeln. Glücklicherweise gibt es viele Möglichkeiten, daran zu arbeiten.

Einige der folgenden Ideen werden dich wahrscheinlich mehr ansprechen als andere. Auch wenn es verlockend sein mag, sich auf diese zu stürzen, solltest du vielleicht ein Zitat des amerikanischen Philosophen Ralph Waldo Emerson berücksichtigen: „Tue immer das, wovor du Angst hast".[16]

Die Strategien, die du ausschließt, könnten die sein, die dir am meisten helfen. Wenn du zum Beispiel davon überzeugt bist, dass dir eine Therapie nichts bringen würde, solltest du dich fragen, ob du „Dinge wegdiskutierst" oder „Informationen ablehnst, die mit deinen bestehenden Glaubenssätzen in Konflikt stehen". Falls dies der Fall sein sollte, lohnt es sich, noch einmal einen Blick in den Abschnitt über kognitive Dissonanz weiter oben in diesem Kapitel zu werfen!

Hier sind die wichtigsten Möglichkeiten, um deine Selbstwahrnehmung in Bezug auf Alkohol zu verbessern, damit du dich mit einer wichtigen Zutat für Veränderungen wappnen kannst – Wissen.

Lernen und neue Erkenntnisse gewinnen

Die Neurowissenschaft hat gezeigt, dass das Gehirn beim Lernen neuer Dinge neue neuronale Bahnen schafft und „bestehende verändern kann".[17] Diese Fähigkeit, den Aufbau des Gehirns ständig zu verändern, wird als Neuroplastizität bezeichnet.

Als ich in der Reha war, hat man uns geraten, neue Kleidung zu kaufen, anders nach Hause zu fahren und die Möbel in unseren Schlafzimmern umzustellen. Dabei ging es darum, unsere Neuroplastizität zu stimulieren und unseren süchtigen Verstand von den vielen Dingen abzulenken, die wir mit Drogen und Alkohol assoziierten. Als ich in die Reha kam, erinnerte mich *alles* an Drogen und Alkohol!

Das war ein guter Rat. Schon eine Fahrt an meiner Stammkneipe vorbei reichte aus, um eine Kette von Ereignissen in Gang zu setzen, die mich fünf Tage später zu Hause ankommen ließen! Als ich anfing, diese Dinge zu ändern, verlor mein Verstand diese Assoziationen (mehr dazu später) und mein Drang, zu trinken und Drogen zu nehmen, wurde mit der Zeit schwächer.

Es ist nie zu spät für dein Gehirn, sich weiterzuentwickeln und dein Unterbewusstsein dazu zu bringen, gesündere Entscheidungen zu treffen. Du erreichst das Erwachsenenalter nicht mit einem voll entwickelten Gehirn. Tatsächlich hört das Gehirn nie auf, sich als Reaktion auf das Lernen zu verändern.

Bücher, Blogartikel, Hörbücher, Online-Kurse, Gruppentherapien, Biografien… all das enthält Wissen, das deine Selbstwahrnehmung stärken kann. Oft geht es nicht darum, mit jedem Wort, das du liest oder hörst, einverstanden zu sein, sondern nur ein oder zwei „Erkenntnisse" aufzuspüren, die dich ansprechen oder dich dazu bringen, deine lang gehegten Glaubenssätze zu hinterfragen.

Du könntest die Memoiren von Sport- oder Musik-Idolen lesen und erfahren, wie sich deren Kindheit auf ihre Entscheidungen als Erwachsene ausgewirkt hat. Vielleicht lernst du dadurch auch etwas Neues über deine eigene Vergangenheit. Du kannst dir auch einen Podcast anhören, den du interessant und ansprechend findest. Du könntest „Quit-Lit"-Bücher und Geschichten über die Sucht lesen und herausfinden, was andere Menschen über sich selbst gelernt haben, als sie mit Alkohol und anderen Drogen aufhörten.

Vielleicht lag dir das Lesen bisher nicht so sehr oder dir fehlt die Geduld dafür. Manche Menschen bevorzugen auditives oder visuelles Lernen. Zum Glück leben wir in einer Welt, in der wir leicht Zugang zu Podcasts, Audible-Hörbüchern und Videos auf Abruf haben. Es gibt also viele Möglichkeiten, Wissen aufzunehmen, neue Nervenbahnen zu aktivieren und Informationen aufzunehmen, die dazu führen, dass wir uns selbst besser wahrnehmen können.

Egal, ob du lieber liest oder zuhörst, Tatsache ist, dass du für etwa 18 Euro oder weniger die Erfahrungen eines ganzen Berufslebens und alle wertvollen Erkenntnisse eines Menschen aufsaugen kannst. Als ehemaliger Finanzberater kann ich mit Sicherheit sagen, dass das Lesen und Zuhören von Büchern die beste Kapitalrendite ist, die du je bekommen wirst!

Wenn du etwas Altes liest, kannst du oft etwas Neues lernen. Du erfährst mehr über die Erfahrungen von Menschen, die ähnliche Probleme wie du überwunden haben. Es kann Spaß machen, herauszufinden, wie deine eigenen persönlichen Helden gelernt haben, erfolgreich zu sein.

Hier ist ein Tipp: Suche dir ein Thema, das dich interessiert, und lies (oder höre) dir drei Bücher der bekanntesten Autoren auf diesem Gebiet an. So bekommst du die besten Erkenntnisse zu jedem Thema – und das zu einem Bruchteil des Preises, der Zeit und der Energie, die es kosten würde, ein Professor auf diesem Gebiet zu werden. Wenn du also für immer mit dem Alkohol aufhören willst, fang an, die Bücher zu lesen und zu hören, die dich dabei unterstützen, auf Alkohol zu verzichten.

Nicht zu unterschätzen sind die lebensverändernden Auswirkungen, die das Erlernen von Neuem auf dein Selbstbewusstsein haben kann, vor allem, wenn es etwas ist, das du schon lange nicht mehr gemacht hast. Uns weiterzubilden macht uns robuster und widerstandsfähiger gegen mögliche Rückfälle.

Feedback einholen

Feedback gehört zu den besten Werkzeugen, die wir haben, um zu verstehen, wie die Menschen uns, unser Verhalten und unsere Arbeit wahrnehmen.

Es gibt nichts, was dich davon abhalten könnte, dieses Feedback direkt einzuholen – von deinen

Freunden, deiner Familie, deinen Chefs und Kollegen.

Natürlich vermeiden es viele Menschen, ein solches Feedback einzuholen – aus Angst, ihr Ego könnte durch etwas Negatives angegriffen werden. Diese Angst kann dazu führen, dass sie nicht nach Feedback fragen oder es ignorieren, um ihr Ego zu schützen.

Wie du dein Ego in den Griff bekommst, werden wir später in diesem Buch genauer besprechen. Für den Moment soll es genügen, dass „lernfähig" zu werden und für Feedback empfänglich zu sein, zu den besten Dingen gehören, die du tun kannst, um deine Selbstwahrnehmung zu stärken.

Bedenke die Alternative: sich weigern zuzuhören, sich nicht weiterentwickeln und im gleichen Kreislauf feststecken.

Wir alle können von anderen lernen – von Menschen mit einschlägiger Erfahrung und Fachwissen (ja, das gilt auch für Menschen, die jünger sind als wir!).

Es gibt keinen Grund zu der Annahme, dass dein Chef sich nicht freuen würde, wenn du ihn fragst, was du tun kannst, um deine Leistung im

Job zu verbessern. Genauso gibt es keinen Grund, warum dein Partner nicht bereit wäre, dir drei Dinge zu nennen, die du tun könntest, um eure Beziehung zu verbessern oder ihr/sein Leben einfacher zu machen! Der Verzicht auf Alkohol könnte eines dieser Dinge sein!

Auf diese Weise „zu lernen", erfordert Mut, doch es ist auch ein fantastischer Weg, um sich selbst besser wahrzunehmen und damit zu beginnen, destruktive Verhaltensweisen zu verlernen und an neuen und besseren zu arbeiten.

Für Feedback empfänglich zu sein führt zu Wachstum und langfristiger Abstinenz.

Reflektiere deine Handlungen und stelle kraftvolle Fragen

Ein guter Weg, um neue Nervenbahnen zu schaffen, ist der Mut, sich selbst tiefgreifende Fragen zu stellen.

Wenn wir regelmäßig trinken, neigen wir dazu, mit anderen Trinkern zu trinken –Menschen, von denen wir uns einreden, dass sie Gleichgesinnte sind. Die Tatsache, dass das Wichtigste, was wir mit diesen Menschen gemeinsam haben, die Vorliebe für Alkohol ist, ist ein Thema für eine ganz andere Diskussion (eine, die du in *Nüchtern auf einem alkoholisierten Planeten - Ohne Alkohol leben* findest).

Wenn du mit Gleichgesinnten zusammen bist, stellst du dir in der Regel nicht die wichtigen Fragen, auf die es ankommt. Fragen wie:

„Wo will ich mit meinem Leben hin?"

„Warum habe ich gestern Abend getrunken?"

„Was ist wirklich los mit mir?"

„Ist ein Kater wirklich ein Zeichen für eine gute Party?"

Es kann herausfordernd und schmerzhaft sein, sich diese Fragen zu stellen und über die Antworten nachzudenken.

Viel einfacher ist es, noch einen Drink zu nehmen.

Es sind die Antworten auf diese Fragen (und andere), die dich auf dem Weg zu mehr Selbstwahrnehmung voranbringen und dir eine echte Chance geben, dich zu verändern. Wenn du dir wichtige Fragen stellst, kannst du anfangen, deine falschen Glaubenssätze zu ändern.

Vielleicht entdeckst du so etwas wie „Alkohol macht mich lustiger" was in Wirklichkeit „Alkohol macht mich leichtsinniger" bedeutet. Vielleicht findest du, dass „Alkohol entspannt", was in Wirklichkeit "macht träge und wenig ehrgeizig" bedeutet.

Wenn du diese Entdeckungen einmal gemacht hast, kannst du sie nicht mehr rückgängig machen. Womit wir wieder dorthin zurückkommen, dass das, was du glaubst, nicht unbedingt richtig ist und zu falschem Handeln führen kann.

Nehmen wir das obige Beispiel, um zu zeigen, wie kraftvolle Fragen in der Praxis funktionieren.

Wenn du tief in deinem Unterbewusstsein davon überzeugt bist, dass Alkohol dich lustig und entspannt macht, wirst du dich sicher immer wieder betrinken. Aber wenn du dir eingestehst, dass er dich rücksichtslos, träge und wenig ehrgeizig macht, triffst du wahrscheinlich ganz andere Entscheidungen.

Das ist eine Selbstwahrnehmung, die das Unterbewusstsein neu vernetzt und Neuroplastizität, mit der du neue Gewohnheiten entwickeln kannst.

Wann warst du das letzte Mal zehn Minuten lang still und hast dir tiefgehende Fragen gestellt? Wenn du mit einem negativen Autopiloten lebst, ist es unwahrscheinlich, dass du dich mal mehr gefragt hast als ein simples: „Warum habe ich das schon wieder gemacht?". Dennoch sind Fragen eine großartige Möglichkeit, unsere Glaubenssätze zu beleuchten und tiefe Selbsterkenntnisse zu erlangen.

Wenn du schon mal mit einem Kleinkind zu tun hattest, kennst du wahrscheinlich die Warum-Phase. Ab dem Zeitpunkt, an dem ein Kind sprechen kann, bis es etwa fünf Jahre alt ist, fragen Kleinkinder unaufhörlich nach dem Warum, um mehr über die Welt um sie herum zu erfahren. Das treibt viele Eltern in den Wahnsinn.

Wenn du deine Selbstwahrnehmung stärken möchtest, sei dieses Kleinkind. Stelle dir immer wieder Fragen und gehe in die Tiefe, bis du nicht mehr weiterkommst.

Wenn du anfängst, die Antworten auf diese wichtigen Fragen zu entdecken, solltest du dir die Antworten zu eigen machen. Es ist wichtig, dass du die Verantwortung für dein Handeln übernimmst, nicht mehr auf andere abwälzt.

Vorwürfe bringen dich nicht an die Wurzel deiner Probleme, sie lenken dich nur ab.

Ein Beispiel:

„Warum habe ich gestern Abend getrunken, obwohl ich weiß, dass ich aufhören möchte?"

Weil ich wütend war und etwas Stress abbauen wollte.

„Warum hat mich die Wut dazu gebracht, Bier zu trinken?"

Weil sechs davon im Kühlschrank standen und mein Blut in Wallung geraten war.

„Warum war ich wütend, bevor ich getrunken habe?"

Weil mein Chef mir gesagt hat, ich solle mich im Job mehr anstrengen.

„Warum hat dich das wütend gemacht?"

Weil ER ein Idiot ist.

Verstehst du, was da passiert?

Du sprichst nicht mehr von „ich", sondern von „er". Jetzt projizierst du deine Antworten (und deine Gründe) auf jemand anderen – deinen Chef.

Damit dieser Prozess effektiv ist, sollst du immer wieder zum „Ich" – zu dir – zurückkehren.

Wenn du dieses Gespräch mit einem Therapeuten führen würdest, würde er dich zu deinem „Ich" zurückbringen und die Fragen fortsetzen:

„Warum macht es dich wütend, wenn dein Chef sagt, dass du bei der Arbeit zu wenig leistest?"

Weil ich weiß, dass ich bei der Arbeit keine Leistung bringe und es nicht mag, wenn man mich darauf anspricht.

„Warum hast du bei der Arbeit keine Leistung gebracht?"

Weil ich immer wieder am Vorabend betrunken bin, mich nicht konzentrieren kann und Hilfe brauche, um nüchtern zu bleiben.

Es kann sogar noch tiefer gehen:

„Warum brauchst du Hilfe, um nüchtern zu bleiben?"

Weil ich nicht in der Lage war, alleine aufzuhören, seit ich mit 14 Jahren angefangen habe, regelmäßig zu trinken.

„Warum hast du mit 14 Jahren regelmäßig getrunken?"

Weil ich den Schmerz, in der Schule gemobbt zu werden, mit der Scheidung meiner Eltern fertig zu werden oder im Unterricht nicht mithalten zu können, loswerden wollte.

An dieser Stelle gäbe es unzählige Beispiele. Je weiter du bereit bist, in den Kaninchenbau vorzudringen, desto mehr stärkst du deine Selbstwahrnehmung. Dabei kannst du einen Punkt erreichen, an dem fast alles in deinem Leben einen Sinn ergibt. Diese Momente werden oft als Offenbarungen, Heureka-Momente oder Geistesblitze bezeichnet.

Diese Momente kommen nicht immer sofort, wenn du dich mit dem Warum beschäftigst. Manchmal dauert es Monate oder sogar Jahre, bis sie sich auflösen. Das Wichtigste ist jedoch, dass du damit anfängst. Wenn du dich mit dem, was du ansprichst, unwohl fühlst, kannst du eine qualifizierte therapeutische Fachkraft aufsuchen, die dich dabei unterstützt.

Selbsterkenntnis hat viele Schichten. Je tiefer du gehst, desto besser sind deine Chancen, deine Probleme zu lösen. Die Arbeit mit dem inneren Kind, zu der wir gleich kommen werden, kann dich auf die tiefste Ebene führen und dir einen echten Heilungsprozess ermöglichen.

Das Stellen kraftvoller Fragen kann dir helfen, wichtige Entscheidungen nicht länger deinem Unterbewusstsein zu überlassen, sondern es „neu zu vernetzen", damit es bessere Entscheidungen trifft!

Wenn es um das Trinken von Alkohol geht, solltest du darauf achten, dass du die Entscheidungen in der Anfangsphase des Aufhörens von deinem Bewusstsein treffen lässt. Auf diese Weise wirst du nicht einfach aus einem Impuls heraus losziehen, sondern kannst die Vor- und Nachteile sowie die möglichen Folgen eines Katers genau durchdenken.

Bedenke: Deine Antworten sind nur so gut wie deine Fragen. Offene Fragen bringen viel mehr ans Licht als geschlossene Fragen.

Zum Thema Alkoholverzicht könntest du dir beispielsweise folgende zwei Fragen stellen:

A. Wogegen sträube ich mich?

B. Wirkt sich Alkohol negativ auf mich aus?

Frage A fordert dich heraus, deine Antworten zu vertiefen. Es ist eine offene Frage. Die zweite Frage ist eine geschlossene Frage und lädt zu einer oberflächlichen „Ja"- oder „Nein"-Antwort ein.

Offene Fragen bringen dich dazu, dich viel mehr damit auseinanderzusetzen. Du bist aufgefordert, darüber nachzudenken und deine Antworten sorgfältig zu analysieren. Je tiefer du gehst, desto mehr Heureka-Momente entdeckst du, desto mehr Punkte kannst du zu einem Bild verbinden und desto mehr falsche Glaubenssätze kannst du hinter dir lassen.

Offene Fragen zu stellen ist eines der ersten Dinge, für die professionelle Therapeuten und Coaches ausgebildet werden. Es ist aber auch eine Fähigkeit, die du selbst entwickeln und auf dich anwenden kannst.

Je mehr Selbstwahrnehmung du hast, desto mehr bewusste Kontrolle kannst du entwickeln. Sei also das Kleinkind und frage dich immer wieder, „Warum?".

Zuhören

Glaubst du, dass du gut zuhören kannst?

Viele Menschen können es nicht. Sie denken viel mehr darüber nach, was sie als Nächstes sagen möchten, als über das, was die andere Person tatsächlich zu ihnen sagt.

Vor über 2.000 Jahren hat schon der stoische Philosoph Epiktet erklärt: „Wir haben zwei Ohren und einen Mund, also können wir doppelt so viel zuhören, wie wir sprechen".[18]

Das ist ein guter Ratschlag - vor allem, wenn du deine Selbstwahrnehmung verbessern willst.

Aktives Zuhören ist eine Kunstform, die Übung erfordert. Es bedeutet, dass du die Worte deines Gesprächspartners auf dich wirken lassen musst, während dein Gehirn sie verarbeitet. Es bedeutet, dass du dich mit unangenehmen Pausen anfreunden musst, statt dich zu beeilen, um zu antworten.

Genau wie beim Lesen von Büchern erhältst du wertvolle Einsichten, wenn du dir die Mühe machst, auf das zu hören, was andere Menschen zu sagen haben. Du profitierst von ihrer Weisheit und ihren Erfahrungen und vielleicht fühlst du dich inspiriert, weitere Fragen zu stellen. Das ist die Kunst des aktiven Zuhörens.

Aktives Zuhören kommt bei jeder Art von Gruppentherapie zum Tragen, auch bei anonymen Gruppentreffen. Es geht darum, auf die Gemeinsamkeiten in diesen Treffen zu hören und sich nicht auf die Unterschiede zu konzentrieren. Wenn du in der Lage bist, die Geschichten, die du hörst, nachzuvollziehen, kann dich das darin bestärken, dass du mit dem Trinken aufhören und nüchtern bleiben kannst.

Wenn du dich in einer Gruppe auf die Unterschiede konzentrierst, lenkt dich dein Ego ab und denkt: „Ich bin nicht wie sie, ich muss ihnen nicht zuhören". Das Ego ist kontraproduktiv für aktives Zuhören, denn die Person könnte eine Fülle hilfreicher Informationen liefern, aber dein Ego redet dir ein, dass du nicht so bist wie sie, und dein Fokus verschiebt sich. Wie du dein Ego zähmen kannst, erfährst du später in diesem Buch.

Frage dich ehrlich, ob du ein guter und aktiver Zuhörer bist. Der amerikanische Psychiater M. Scott Peck sagte: „Man kann niemandem wirklich zuhören und gleichzeitig etwas anderes tun".[19] Wenn du also oft feststellst, dass deine

Gedanken mitten im Gespräch abschweifen, versuche daran zu arbeiten. Es lohnt sich.

Raus aus der Komfortzone (und rein in das gesunde Risiko)

Ein todsicherer Weg, mehr über sich selbst zu erfahren (und sich seiner selbst bewusster zu werden), ist eine neue Umgebung zu erkunden, neue Dinge zu tun und neue Menschen kennenzulernen.

Das ist besonders wertvoll, wenn dein „normaler" Umgang nicht gut für dich ist oder dich zurückhält.

Du kannst diese Strategie in einem Satz zusammenfassen: „Gewöhne dich an das Ungewöhnliche!" Nüchternsein bedeutet, neue Dinge, neue Umgebungen und neue Menschen zu erleben.

Es gibt keinen Grund, sich davon einschüchtern zu lassen. Alle tun was sie tun irgendwann ein erstes Mal – oft mit dem motivierenden Gefühl, es geschafft zu haben und Lust auf das nächste Mal oder die nächste Sache zu bekommen.

Nüchternheit setzt Zeit, Geld und Energie frei, um all die Dinge zu tun, die du schon immer mal machen wolltest oder „nicht geschafft hast". Und jedes Mal, wenn du eines dieser Dinge tust, hast du die Gelegenheit, innezuhalten und über die neue Erfahrung zu reflektieren. Wie hat es sich angefühlt? Wie hast du dich in dieser neuen Situation verhalten? Würdest du es gerne wieder tun?

Was geben dir die Antworten auf diese Fragen? Mehr Selbsterkenntnis!

Besuche eine Gruppentherapie, buche einen Tandem-Fallschirmsprung, beginne einen Abendkurs und nimm die Hobbys wieder auf, die dich als Kind begeistert haben. Nüchternheit gibt dir all diese Möglichkeiten, und alles, was du erlebst, fließt in eine positive Feedbackschleife ein:

Entwickle deine Selbstwahrnehmung > ergreife positive Maßnahmen > verbessere deine Intuition für das, was dich wirklich glücklich macht. Wiederhole das Ganze, um beste Ergebnisse zu erzielen.

Therapie und die Arbeit mit dem inneren Kind

Wenn du bereit bist, dich selbst besser kennenzulernen und eine ausgeprägte

Selbstwahrnehmung zu entwickeln (was ich dir sehr empfehle), lohnt es sich, die Zusammenarbeit mit einem professionellen Therapeuten in Betracht zu ziehen.

Das ist vor allem dann wichtig, wenn du in denselben Denk- oder Verhaltensmustern festzustecken scheinst. Dann ist es möglicherweise an der Zeit, eine therapeutische Fachkraft zu Rate zu ziehen.

Wenn du einen Punkt erreicht hast, an dem du darüber nachdenkst, mit einem Therapeuten oder einer Therapeutin zu arbeiten, ist das etwas Gutes. Es zeigt, dass du dich selbst schon gut genug kennst, um zu erkennen, dass du „feststeckst". Manche Menschen tun sich schwer, an diesen Punkt zu gelangen und wehren sich vehement dagegen, sich zu öffnen.

Dadurch bleiben sie stecken und kommen nicht weiter. Wenn du bereit bist, dir einzugestehen, dass du Hilfe brauchst, hast du schon gewonnen.

Lass dich nicht von deinen falschen Glaubenssätzen zurückhalten, wenn du Hilfe brauchst. Ich bin mit dem Irrglauben aufgewachsen, dass es eine Schwäche ist, um Hilfe zu bitten. Wie falsch ich doch lag! Mir endlich einzugestehen, dass ich Hilfe brauche, und eine Therapie zu beginnen, war das Beste, das ich je gemacht habe.

Es ist ganz natürlich, dass wir uns in unserem Leben und in täglichen Drucksituationen einfügen. Außerdem sind viele unserer Glaubenssätze – auch die nicht hilfreichen – tief verwurzelt.

Therapeuten haben eine jahrelange Ausbildung absolviert, um Menschen dabei zu unterstützen, sich ihrer selbst bewusst zu werden und sich von ihren Problemen zu lösen.

Sie sind gute Zuhörer. Du wirst feststellen, dass sie dir oft wiedergeben, was du denkst – und zwar besser, als du es selbst ausdrücken könntest!

Gute Therapeut/innen stellen dir Fragen, die dir sonst niemand stellen würde. Ihre Aufgabe ist es, dich dabei zu unterstützen, zu verstehen, warum du tust, was du tust. Es ist nicht ihre Aufgabe, dir zu sagen, was du tun sollst. Es ist wesentlich wirkungsvoller, wenn du am Ende jeder Sitzung zu deinen eigenen Schlussfolgerungen kommst, als darauf zu warten, dass dir gesagt wird, welche Schlüsse du ziehen solltest.

Therapeut/innen unterstützen dich auch bei der Arbeit mit dem inneren Kind, die ich bereits erwähnt habe. Es ist wichtig, das ganze „Erzähl mir von deinem Vater"-Klischee zu ignorieren. Viele Therapieansätze, wie z. B. die kognitive Verhaltenstherapie oder die Adlersche Psychologie, arbeiten nicht auf diese Weise. Dennoch haben deine frühen Erfahrungen oft einen großen Einfluss darauf, warum du tust, was du tust, und warum du so fühlst, wie du fühlst. Gute Therapeut/innen werden dich dabei unterstützen.

Menschen sagen oft, dass sie eine „schöne Kindheit" hatten, können sich dann aber nicht an viel aus dieser Zeit erinnern. Was für sie damals traumatisch war, erscheint ihnen heute vielleicht gar nicht mehr so.

Die Wirkung von Erkenntnissen aus deiner Vergangenheit kann nicht oft genug betont werden. So könntest du zum Beispiel herausfinden, dass du das Opfer eines Verhaltens warst, das du als „akzeptabel" betrachtet hast, obwohl es in Wirklichkeit nicht so war. Vielleicht entdeckst du einen bestimmten Wendepunkt, der dein Selbstvertrauen und dein Selbstwertgefühl erschüttert hat. Vielleicht erinnerst du dich sogar an ein Trauma, das du bisher „verdrängt" hast, weil es zu schmerzhaft war, um es zu verarbeiten.

Tiefe Wunden müssen tief gereinigt werden. Andernfalls schleicht sich eine Infektion ein, und der Schmerz kehrt mit aller Macht zurück. So ist es auch mit der Sucht. Wie eingangs erwähnt, weißt du, was du tust, aber der Schlüssel zu einer dauerhaften Veränderung liegt darin herauszufinden, *warum* du es tust.

Beim regelmäßigen Trinken geht es oft darum, unangenehme Gefühle zu verdrängen. Allerdings tauchen sie immer wieder auf, wenn du dich nicht mit der Ursache auseinandersetzt.

„Indem wir das Kind sanft halten, beruhigen wir unsere schwierigen Emotionen und können anfangen, uns wohlzufühlen. Wenn wir unsere starken Emotionen mit Achtsamkeit und Konzentration umarmen, können wir die Wurzeln dieser mentalen Strukturen erkennen. Wir wissen dann, woher unser Leiden kommt. Wenn wir die Wurzeln der Dinge sehen, verringert sich unser Leiden." *Thich Nhat Hanh.*[20]

Wenn du eine Therapie ausprobieren möchtest, was ich wärmstens empfehle, findest du hier ein paar Tipps, wie du den oder die richtige Therapeut/in für dich findest:

- Führe ein Gespräch mit zwei oder drei Personen, bevor du dich entscheidest. Manchmal stimmt die Chemie einfach nicht. Du hast bestimmt ein gutes Gespür dafür, ob eine Person „gut passt".

- Versuche, eine therapeutische Fachkraft zu finden, die mindestens ein paar Jahre Berufserfahrung hat. Persönliche Erfahrungen können ebenso wichtig sein, wobei eine gute Therapeutin oder ein guter Therapeut nicht unbedingt ihre/seine Vergangenheit preisgeben wird, denn das kann Auswirkungen darauf haben, wie ihr miteinander umgeht.

- Entscheide dich für eine Person, der du vertraust. Ohne Vertrauen sind wir nicht in der Lage, uns vollständig zu öffnen. Wenn wir uns nicht vollständig öffnen, können wir nicht tief genug vordringen, um effektiv zu heilen.

- Achte darauf, dass der Therapeut oder die Therapeutin angemessen qualifiziert ist. Eine Ausbildung zur therapeutischen Fachkraft dauert Jahre und umfasst viele Stunden an beaufsichtigten Sitzungen. Je mehr Erfahrung, desto besser, aber wahrscheinlich auch teurer.

Dir einen Therapeuten oder eine Therapeutin zu suchen, kann zu den wichtigsten Dingen gehören, die du in deinem Leben tust – das ist absolute Selbstfürsorge. Lege deine falschen Glaubenssätze beiseite und probiere es einfach aus.

„Selbsttherapie" mit Journaling

Journaling ist nicht ganz dasselbe wie das Durcharbeiten deiner Probleme mit Hilfe einer ausgebildeten therapeutischen Fachkraft. Es ist jedoch ein sehr wirkungsvolles Instrument, das oft zusätzlich zu Therapiesitzungen empfohlen wird.

Damit kannst du sofort anfangen. Alles, was du brauchst, sind ein Notizbuch und einen Stift. Es gibt auch eine ganze Reihe von Journalen, die du zu erschwinglichen Preisen kaufen kannst.

Eine nützliche Methode ist das tägliche Notieren einiger Reflexionen – sowohl morgens als auch abends. So erhältst du ein sichtbares Muster dafür, wie sich deine Stimmung jeden Tag verändert.

Mit diesen Informationen kannst du analysieren, was zwischen diesen beiden Zeiträumen passiert ist und wie sich das auf deine Gefühle ausgewirkt hat. (Denke daran, dass es deine Gefühle sind, die deine Handlungen bestimmen.)

Mit der Zeit wirst du so deine emotionale Intelligenz aufbauen, auf die wir in einem späteren Kapitel näher eingehen werden.

Sich die Zeit zu nehmen, aufzuschreiben, was dir durch den Kopf geht, ist an sich schon therapeutisch. Die Worte, die in deinem Journal landen, sind der Schlüssel zu allen möglichen tiefgründigeren Einsichten. Sie unterstützen dich dabei, dich besser kennenzulernen und deine Selbstwahrnehmung zu stärken. Du kannst dich fragen, was du besser hättest machen können und ehrlich über die Dinge sprechen, die an diesem Tag nicht so gut gelaufen sind. Auf der anderen Seite kannst du reflektieren, was funktioniert hat und was dir Freude bereitet hat.

Es gibt eine Vielzahl von Journalen, die sich mit der Alkoholabstinenz beschäftigen. Probiere einfach ein paar von den gut bewerteten aus und denke daran, dass Beständigkeit der Schlüssel zu den besten Ergebnissen ist. Das Schreiben von ein Jounal kann dir dabei helfen, dein inneres Narrativ von negativ zu positiv zu verändern. Die Wiederholung von Dankbarkeit, Reflexionen am Morgen und am Abend sowie positive Affirmationen (dazu später mehr) werden dazu führen, dass sich die inneren Gespräche, die du mit dir selbst führst, verändern. Wenn du anfängst, positiv mit dir selbst zu sprechen, spiegelt sich das in deinen Handlungen und in der Art, wie du die Welt siehst, wider.

Unterschätze nie, wie wirkungsvoll das Schreiben von Tagebüchern oder Journalen sein kann, um mit dem Alkohol aufzuhören, nüchtern zu bleiben und eine positive Einstellung zu bewahren.

Meditation und Achtsamkeit

Meditation und Achtsamkeit sind fabelhafte Werkzeuge, um deine Selbstwahrnehmung zu entwickeln. Eine aktuelle Studie schätzt, dass rund 275 Millionen Menschen auf der ganzen Welt meditieren.[21] Können so viele Menschen falsch liegen?!

Obwohl Meditation und Achtsamkeit oft in einem Atemzug genannt werden und eng miteinander verwandt sind, ist es wichtig, den Unterschied zwischen den beiden zu kennen, um die Praktiken auszuwählen, von denen du am meisten profitieren wirst. Der Unterschied ist folgendermaßen zu verstehen: „Achtsamkeit ist eine Fähigkeit, wobei die Meditation eine Praxis ist.".[22] Dennoch praktizieren viele Menschen Meditation, *um an ihrer Achtsamkeit zu arbeiten.*

Ein hervorragendes erstes Ziel ist es, eine regelmäßige Praxis zu entwickeln, die für dich funktioniert und es dir ermöglicht, intensiv zu meditieren. In diesem meditativen Zustand kannst du beginnen, Situationen in deinem Leben zu beobachten, sie zu verarbeiten, deine körperliche und geistige Anspannung zu lösen und sie loszulassen.

Im Gegensatz dazu leidest du vielleicht unter immer wiederkehrenden, kreisenden Gedanken in deinem täglichen Leben. Bei regelmäßigen Trinkern sind das oft Gedanken wie „Wie habe ich mich gestern Abend auf der Arbeit verhalten?" oder „Wie kann ich es bei meiner Familie wieder gutmachen, dass ich am Weihnachtstag verkatert war?"

Die Atmung ist ein weiteres kraftvolles Instrument, und es ist kein Wunder, dass sie bei Praktiken wie Yoga und Meditation eine wichtige Rolle spielt. Atemübungen verbessern den Vagustonus, erhöhen unsere emotionale Kontrolle, reduzieren Angst und Stress und verringern chronische Entzündungen im Körper.[23]

Meditation schafft die Zeit und den Raum, in dem du die Dinge aus einer klareren Perspektive betrachten kannst. Im Gegenzug wirst du im Alltag allmählich achtsamer und kannst zukünftigen Situationen mit einem besseren Urteilsvermögen und mehr Klarheit begegnen. Außerdem lernst du dadurch kleine Übungen, die du im Laufe des Tages anwenden kannst, wenn du mit Stress, Herausforderungen und schwierigen Entscheidungen konfrontiert bist.

Bewegung und Ernährung

Selbstwahrnehmung ist nicht nur eine geistige, sondern auch eine körperliche Angelegenheit.

Die Nahrung, die wir zu uns nehmen, und die Bewegung, die wir ausüben (oder nicht), haben einen großen Einfluss auf unsere Stimmung und unseren Gemütszustand. Im weiteren Verlauf des Buches werden wir uns mit der Darm-Hirn-Achse befassen und damit, wie sie deinen alkoholfreien Weg maßgeblich beeinflusst.

Es braucht jedoch keine Wissenschaft, um zu erkennen, dass bestimmte Dinge wahr sind. Es genügt, wenn du dich fragst, wie du dich fühlen würdest, wenn du dich eine Woche lang in einem Raum einschließen würdest, ohne Sport und ausschließlich mit fettigem, bestelltem Essen.

Ernährung und Bewegung sind wichtig.

Bewegung ist ein transformatives Werkzeug, das du aktiv nutzen kannst, um deine Gefühle zu regulieren. Eine Studie hat gezeigt, dass „Personen, die Sport treiben, um ihre Stimmung zu verbessern, höhere Werte bei der emotionalen Intelligenz aufweisen."[24]

Menschen trinken oft Alkohol und nehmen Drogen, um ihre Gefühle zu regulieren. Die Tatsache, dass du diese Zeilen liest, deutet darauf hin, dass du den Punkt erreicht hast, an dem du erkennst, dass das nicht funktioniert. Besser zu essen und Sport zu treiben, funktioniert sehr wohl.

Sicherlich hast du schon oft bereut, dass du unter der Woche ausgegangen bist oder die zweite Flasche Wein geöffnet hast. Aber hast du es wirklich schon einmal bereut, ins Fitnessstudio gegangen zu sein, dich im

Spinning-Kurs angestrengt zu haben oder einen schlechten Tag auf der Arbeit mit einem Lauf hinter dir gelassen zu haben?

Was hat das alles mit Selbstwahrnehmung zu tun?

Je mehr du über Bewegung und Ernährung lernst und je mehr du nach dem, was du lernst, handelst, desto mehr wirst du *intuitiv* verstehen, was dein Geist und dein Körper brauchen. Das ist Selbstwahrnehmung.

Mit der Zeit verstehst du – auf einer tieferen Ebene – wie sehr Körper und Geist miteinander verbunden sind. Das kann sich ins Unterbewusstsein einprägen und deine weniger gesunden Bewältigungsstrategien verdrängen. Vielleicht hast du bald das Gefühl, dass du es „brauchst", Gewichte zu heben, anstatt einen Drink zu „brauchen"!

Wenn du erkennst, dass deine geistige Gesundheit direkt mit deiner körperlichen Gesundheit zusammenhängt, bist du in der Lage, deine Stimmung zu jedem Zeitpunkt zu verändern. Bewegung ist Medizin und führt zu einer ganz anderen Feedbackschleife als die Selbstmedikation mit Alkohol (die nie gut endet).

***

Wenn du in deiner Nüchternheit nicht an deiner Selbstwahrnehmung arbeitest, machst du nicht die Hausaufgaben, die nötig sind, um zu überwinden, warum du überhaupt getrunken hast. Leider ist das der Grund, warum viele Menschen „feststecken" oder eine Zeit lang nicht trinken, bevor sie wieder in ihre alten Muster (oder Schlimmeres) zurückfallen.

Wenn du dir deiner selbst bewusst wirst, kannst du das, was du gelernt hast, in die Tat umsetzen und so mit dem Trinken aufhören und nüchtern bleiben.

Bevor du zum nächsten Kapitel übergehst, möchte ich dir eine kurze Übung vorschlagen, die auf den zuvor erwähnten wichtigen Fragen basiert.

Stelle dir diese einfache Frage:

„Warum bin ich hier?"

Reise so weit wie möglich in den Kaninchenbau und denke daran, dein inneres 4-jähriges Kind zu aktivieren. Lass auf jede Antwort eine weitere „Warum?"-Frage folgen und achte darauf, dass jede Antwort mit „Ich ..." beginnt.

Bedenke: Wissen ist nur *potenzielle* Stärke. Im nächsten Kapitel machen wir uns diese Stärke zunutze, indem wir lernen, positiv zu handeln.

Bedenke: Wissen ist nur *potenzielle* Stärke. Im nächsten Kapitel machen wir uns diese Stärke zunutze, indem wir lernen, positiv zu handeln.

Kapitel 2:

Träume ohne Ziele sind nur Träume: Ziele, positives Handeln und Intuition

Was sind deine Ziele im Leben? Gehen sie über das bloße Überleben bis zum nächsten Tag, dem nächsten Wochenende, dem nächsten Gehaltstag oder der nächsten arbeitsfreien Woche hinaus?

Wer regelmäßig trinkt, hat oft keine wirklichen Ziele. Im Leben geht es dann nur noch darum, durchzukommen:

- verkatert durch den Tag/die Tage auf der Arbeit kommen
- den „langweiligen Teil" des gesellschaftlichen Ereignisses überstehen, bis es Zeit ist, etwas trinken zu gehen

- mit dem verbleibenden Überziehungsrahmen bis zum Ende des Monats durchhalten
- bis zum nächsten Urlaub durchhalten – weil du ein Leben führst, dem du nur entfliehen willst.

Unabhängig von deinen persönlichen Lebensumständen, deiner finanziellen Situation oder dem Stand deiner Karriere ist das ein ziemlich trostloses Dasein. Niemand strebt wirklich danach, nur zu überleben.

Wie wir bereits festgestellt haben, besteht das Problem darin, dass das Trinken den negativen Kreislauf „trinken > verkatert sein > demotiviert sein > wenig Energie > wieder trinken" ankurbelt.

Kein Wunder, dass uns das davon abhält, auf konkrete Ziele hinzuarbeiten. Es ist möglich, jahrelang in diesem Teufelskreis stecken zu bleiben. Mir ging es so.

Dann ist da die plötzliche Erkenntnis, dass das Leben ohne nennenswerte Erfolge vor deinen Augen vorbeizieht. Als „Legende", „Schwergewicht" oder „der Letzte, der noch aufrecht stehen kann" bekannt zu sein, zählt nicht. Wenn du mehr trinkst als deine Freunde, bekommst du dafür weder eine Medaille noch eine Urkunde!

Falls du nach Inspiration suchst, um dir sinnvolle Ziele zu setzen, denke über dieses Zitat des stoischen Philosophen (und römischen Kaisers) Marcus Aurelius nach:

„Betrachte dich als tot. Du hast dein Leben gelebt. Jetzt nimm das, was übrig ist, und lebe es richtig."[25]

Deshalb solltest du dir nüchterne Ziele setzen

Das obige Zitat ist sicherlich eine harte Nummer, allerdings lässt sich seine Weisheit nicht leugnen. Sich Ziele zu setzen, hilft dir, neue Verhaltensweisen zu entwickeln, deinen Fokus zu lenken und dein Leben in Schwung zu bringen. Es ist das genaue Gegenteil von dem, was der Alkohol für dich getan hat: Er hat dich zu denselben vorhersehbaren Verhaltensweisen geführt, du hattest keinerlei Fokus außerhalb des Alkoholkonsums und bist im Leben nicht voran gekommen.

Ziele können klein und trivial oder groß und bedeutend sein. Sie können kurz-, mittel- oder langfristig sein. Das Erreichen der kleinen Ziele führt dazu, dass du die großen Ziele erreichst. Fast immer sind es die kurzfristigen Ziele, die dich darauf vorbereiten, die langfristigen Ziele zu erreichen.

Das kurzfristige Ziel, „mit dem Trinken aufhören", könnte beispielsweise der erste Schritt zu dem größeren Ziel „inneren Frieden finden" sein.

Die in anonymen Gruppen weit verbreitete Einstellung „nur für heute" ist ein mächtiges Werkzeug, das dir hilft, deine Ziele zu erreichen. Mitglieder der Anonymen Alkoholiker tragen oft einen Schlüsselanhänger oder eine Medaille mit der Aufschrift „Nur für heute" bei sich, um sich daran zu erinnern. Es geht darum, sich auf die Gegenwart zu konzentrieren und keine Zeit und Energie auf die Vergangenheit oder Zukunft zu verwenden.

Etwas zu erreichen, fühlt sich gut an und setzt eine gesunde Feedbackschleife in Gang. Hast du schon mal beschlossen, eine Fläche in der Küche abzuwischen und dann den ganzen Raum auf Vordermann gebracht oder eine Schublade ausgeräumt und dich dann motiviert gefühlt, auch alle anderen zu erledigen?

Wenn du mit dem Trinken aufhören möchtest, ist das Setzen von überschaubaren Zielen wichtig, genauso wie bei allen anderen Dingen im Leben. Du beginnst mit einer einzigen sauberen, blitzblanken Oberfläche und hast am Ende ein blitzblankes Zuhause. Fang klein an und nutze die Motivation und das Erfolgserlebnis, um immer weiter voranzukommen.

Wir werden uns gleich damit beschäftigen, wie du dir Ziele setzt und darauf hinarbeitest. Doch zunächst ist es wichtig, daran zu denken, dass du dich für das Erreichen großer und kleiner Ziele belohnen kannst (und solltest). Belohne dich nur nicht mit einem alkoholischen Getränk!

Wenn du einen Welpen trainierst, gibst du ihm ein Leckerli, wenn er das gewünschte positive Verhalten zeigt, z. B., wenn er draußen auf die Toilette geht und nicht in der Wohnung! Nach einer Weile erinnern sie sich an diese positiven Verhaltensweisen und zeigen sie ganz natürlich. Sie verknüpfen das Verhalten mit der Belohnung.

Ich will damit nicht sagen, dass menschliches Verhalten nicht viel komplizierter und nuancierter ist als das Verhalten von Welpen! Aber es IST sehr wohl ähnlich. Es ist nur so, dass der Konsum von Alkohol es viel komplizierter macht, als es sein müsste.

Denk mal darüber nach, wie die Grundlagen dieses Belohnungsmechanismus verdreht werden, wenn wir gewohnheitsmäßig trinken. Wir belohnen „glücklich" mit einem Drink. Wir belohnen „traurig" mit einem Drink. Wir belohnen „deprimiert" mit einem Drink. Wir belohnen „wütend" mit einem Drink. Wir belohnen „gestresst" mit einem Drink.

Es ist, als würde man einen Welpen für *alle möglichen* Verhaltensweisen belohnen – mit einem ungesunden Leckerli – und sich dann wundern, warum er jeden Tag Chaos anrichtet. (Ich kenne das, ich habe selbst einen Welpen!)

Der Alkohol-Belohnungs-Mechanismus läuft schon so lange, dass er auf Autopilot läuft. Wenn du diese Verbindung *bewusst wahrnimmst* und *positiv handelst,* indem du dich mit etwas anderem als Alkohol belohnst, kannst du deine Neuroplastizität verändern und neue, gesündere Belohnungsgewohnheiten entwickeln.

Später im Buch sprechen wir über emotionale Intelligenz. Jedes Gefühl mit Alkohol zu „belohnen", ist ein zuverlässiger Weg, deine emotionale Intelligenz zu zerstören. Damit belohnst du dich dafür, dass du Gefühle unterdrückst. Du lernst nicht, auf gesunde Art und Weise mit ihnen umzugehen.

Unter den Folgen wirst du wahrscheinlich viel mehr leiden als ein Welpe!

Ein SMARTer Weg, mit dem Trinken aufzuhören

Vielleicht hast du schon von der SMART-Methode für das Setzen von Zielen gehört. Sie wird oft im Arbeitsleben verwendet, kann dir aber auch bei der Festlegung von Zielen in allen anderen Bereichen helfen.

Das Ziel dieses Buches ist, dass du aufhörst, Alkohol zu trinken und nüchtern bleibst. Aufgeschlüsselt bedeutet das, dass du das kurzfristige Ziel, nüchtern zu bleiben, jeden Tag erreichst. (Wenn du körperlich alkoholabhängig bist und unter Entzugserscheinungen leidest, kann es sein, dass du deinen Alkoholkonsum zunächst auf Null reduzieren musst. Bitte sprich mit einer medizinischen Fachkraft über die beste Art der Entgiftung in deinem Fall, wenn du deinen Alkoholkonsum reduzieren musst.)

SMART steht für:

- **S**PEZIFISCH
- **M**ESSBAR
- **A**TTRAKTIV
- **R**EALISTISCH
- **T**ERMINIERT

Wenden wir dies auf das Ziel an, mit dem Alkoholkonsum aufzuhören.

SPEZIFISCH:

Trinke 24 Stunden lang keinen Alkohol.

Spezifisch zu sein ist wichtig, damit wir uns unsere Ziele vorstellen können. Das ist besonders wertvoll, wenn du mit dem Trinken aufhörst. Bedenke: „Mit dem Trinken aufhören" hat in unseren Gedanken nicht das gleiche Gewicht wie „in den nächsten 24 Stunden keinen Alkohol trinken".

Je klarer unsere Ziele, desto leichter sind sie zu erreichen. In diesem konkreten Beispiel trägt auch die Tatsache, dass Wiederholungen zu Gewohnheiten führen und dass wir aus dem Kreislauf von Leistung und Belohnung lernen, zur Weiterentwicklung des kurzfristigen Ziels in Richtung des langfristigen Ziels bei.

MESSBAR:

Was du nicht messen kannst, kannst du auch nicht überprüfen oder verbessern. Das gilt für Nüchternheit genauso wie für die persönliche Entwicklung.

Es ist einfach zu messen, ob du Alkohol trinkst oder nicht. Es gibt jedoch verschiedene Möglichkeiten, wie du dich selbst zur Verantwortung ziehen kannst. Du könntest dich zum Beispiel einer Suchtgruppe anschließen – online oder offline. Du könntest eine App herunterladen und deine nüchternen Tage dokumentieren, oder du könntest eine therapeutische Fachkraft oder einen Coach engagieren und ihnen gegenüber Rechenschaft ablegen.

Du kannst dich sogar in die sozialen Medien wagen und eine Seite für anonyme Nüchternheit einrichten, um dich mit anderen zu vernetzen, die auf einem ähnlichen Weg sind, und um dich selbst zur Verantwortung zu ziehen. Suche nach @nüchtern- oder @alkoholfrei-Accounts, denen du folgen und dich von ihnen inspirieren lassen kannst (oder auch nicht!). Sei nur vorsichtig, dass du nicht auf die „Likes" hereinfällst, die dein Ego nähren (dazu später mehr).

Zu sehen, wie sich der nüchterne Tag aufbaut, ist an sich schon lohnend, und jeden nüchternen Meilenstein zu feiern, hilft, die Motivation für den nächsten zu steigern.

ATTRAKTIV:

Mit dem Trinken aufzuhören IST *erstrebenswert* und machbar.

VIELE Menschen hören jedes Jahr auf zu trinken. Darunter sind einige, die mehr verloren haben als du, die mehr getrunken haben als du, die mehr Streitereien, mehr Auseinandersetzungen und mehr Kater hatten.

Das soll die Situation, in der du dich befindest, nicht schmälern – aber es steht außer Frage, dass es *attraktiv* und machbar ist, mit dem Trinken aufzuhören, unabhängig davon, wo du dich heute befindest.

REALISTISCH:

Ist das Ziel, das Trinken aufzugeben und nüchtern zu bleiben, *realistisch*? Ja!

Du hast dieses Buch mit der Absicht in die Hand genommen, dein Leben positiv zu verändern.

Du befindest dich nicht mehr in der „sollte"-Phase. Du bist hier und du bist bereit.

Das Ziel IST *realistisch*.

TERMINIERT:

Wie bereits erwähnt, kannst du den Zeitrahmen ganz einfach halten: 24 Stunden – ein Tag nach dem anderen.

Auch wenn es toll wäre, sich das Ziel zu setzen, 365 Tage lang nüchtern zu bleiben, ist es für unseren Verstand viel einfacher, sich 24 Stunden lang darauf zu fokussieren, nicht zu trinken. Auch hier wollen wir uns darin üben, ganz präsent zu sein. Dabei hilft es uns, es bei einem Tag zu belassen.

Eine Reise über 1000 Kilometer beginnt mit einem einzigen Schritt. Das Gleiche gilt für das Nüchternsein.

Alle Wege zu einem nüchternen Leben beginnen mit einem einzigen Tag ohne Alkohol.

Ziele für die Nüchternheit vs. Trinkziele

Weiter vorne in diesem Kapitel habe ich festgestellt, dass viele Trinkende nicht wirklich konkrete Ziele haben.

Das war bei mir nicht unbedingt der Fall.

Ich hatte das Ziel, jedes Jahr nach Ibiza zu fahren – um der Tatsache zu entfliehen, dass ich meinen Job wirklich nicht mochte!

Innerhalb dieses übergeordneten Ziels hatte ich auch Unterziele für meinen Urlaub - die Ziele, die die Gesellschaft von einem alleinstehenden Mann in seinen Zwanzigern erwartet:

- Einen gebräunten, durchtrainierten Körper zu bekommen (ist jedes Mal gescheitert – der Alkohol kam mir in die Quere).
- Mit vielen Leuten vögeln (ist jedes Mal gescheitert, wenn mir der Alkohol in die Quere kam!)
- So viele Drogen wie möglich zu nehmen (das ist gelungen).
- Mit einem besch******* Gefühl zurückkommen (das war nie ein

wirkliches Ziel, aber ich habe es trotzdem immer erreicht).

Seit ich nüchtern bin, habe ich immer Dinge, die ich im Urlaub erreichen möchte. Mein Hauptziel ist es, keinen Alkohol zu trinken und mit aufgeladenen Batterien und verjüngt zurückzukommen, um meine nächsten Ziele in Angriff zu nehmen. Dazu gehört immer, nüchtern zu sein, Ziele im Beruf, in der Beziehung und alle anderen Ziele, die mich morgens aus dem Bett locken.

Ich habe eine Menge Urlaubstage (und eine Menge Geld) verschwendet, weil ich mich nach dem Urlaub schlechter fühlte als vor meiner Abreise.

Die Ziele, die ich jetzt habe, geben mir einen Sinn – etwas, das ich nie auf dem Boden einer Flasche oder in einer leeren Kokainpackung finden konnte. Nüchtern zu sein und Ziele zu haben, hat mir ermöglicht, nicht nur an den Wochenenden, sondern auch von Montag bis Freitag einen Sinn zu finden.

Nicht nur das Wochenende ist zum Leben da, sondern der Montagmorgen genauso wie der Freitagabend!

Millionen von Yogis auf der ganzen Welt machen etwas Ähnliches. Sie legen zu Beginn der Yogapraxis ihre Absichten fest. Es ist ein Werkzeug, das das Bewusstsein für die bevorstehende Aufgabe fördert, sie zur Verantwortung zieht und ihnen ein Ziel gibt. Bedenke: Hast du schon einmal einen unglücklichen Yogi getroffen?

So erreichst du durch positives Handeln deine Ziele

Positives Handeln bedeutet, dass du deinen Zielen näher kommst.

Hier ist ein Beispiel für positives Handeln sowie eine negative Alternative:

- Sag „Nein" zum Trinken heute Abend, und du wirst morgen früh frisch und munter aufwachen und deine Familie besuchen können.
- Sag „Ja" zu „nur einem Drink" heute Abend, und aus dem einen Drink werden wahrscheinlich sechs. Du wachst morgen früh auf und fühlst dich wie der Tod, sagst das Familientreffen ab und hast den Rest der Woche ein schlechtes Gewissen.

Leider gibt es keine magische „Geheimzutat", die dich plötzlich dazu bringt, die richtigen Entscheidungen zu treffen. Motivation *entsteht* durch Handeln – und unvollkommenes Handeln ist besser als perfekte Untätigkeit.

Ein Personal Trainer würde dir wahrscheinlich sagen: „Am schwersten ist es, deinen Hintern von der Couch zu bekommen!" Das Gleiche gilt für den Verzicht auf Alkohol – du musst dich anstrengen. Niemand kommt, um dich zu retten.

Hier kommt wieder die kognitive Dissonanz ins Spiel. Viele Menschen wollen Sport treiben und wissen um die vielen Vorteile. Aber sie trainieren nicht und haben dann ein schlechtes Gewissen deswegen. Auch beim Trinken wissen viele, dass es ihnen besser gehen würde, wenn sie auf Alkohol verzichten. Oft gibt über Jahre hinweg genügend Belege dafür, dass die Wahrscheinlichkeit, dass es „nur ein oder zwei" sind, gleich null ist. Aber sie tun es trotzdem und haben dann tagelang ein schlechtes Gewissen, voller Schuldgefühle und Reue.

Der Weg, diese kognitive Dissonanz zu überwinden, ist keine Raketenwissenschaft. Es geht darum, die richtigen positiven Maßnahmen zu ergreifen: ins Fitnessstudio zu gehen oder „nein" zu sagen, wenn du abends ausgehst.

Dadurch werden neue Nervenbahnen aktiviert, die dir dabei helfen, dich von deinem alten Trinkverhalten zu lösen und ein gesünderes Verhalten zu entwickeln.

Eins führt dann zum anderen und alles wird leichter – und zwar schnell. Es geht lediglich um Beständigkeit. Wenn du das erste Mal frisch aufstehst, den Tag genießt und ein paar Dinge erledigst, fängst du an, diesen neuen, gesunden Kreislauf aufzubauen. Es wird sich gut anfühlen. Du wirst es wieder tun *wollen*.

Ich behaupte nicht, dass das ein Kinderspiel ist. Mit der Zeit wird dein Gehirn auf Vermeidung getrimmt. Es trickst und manipuliert dich, damit du das Einfache tust, und das ist in der Regel das, was du dir angewöhnt hast zu tun. Es ist sicher nicht das, was außerhalb deiner Komfortzone liegt.

Aber erinnere dich an das Mantra „nur für heute“. Das ist alles, was du brauchst, um anzufangen – die Bereitschaft, das erste Mal das Richtige zu tun.

Es ist völlig in Ordnung, etwas falsch zu machen. Wir alle machen Fehler, auch wenn unsere Absichten positiv sind. Aber wir haben eine wichtige Wahl: Wir können entweder aus den

Fehlern lernen oder sie ignorieren (und uns darauf einstellen, sie immer wieder zu machen). Da du dieses Buch liest, hast du wahrscheinlich schon genug davon, dich für die zweite Option zu entscheiden.

Ich möchte dich ermutigen, eine Liste mit positiven Maßnahmen zu erstellen, die dich deinem Ziel, mit dem Trinken aufzuhören, näher bringen (oder einem anderen Ziel auf deinem Weg, wenn du bereits mit dem Trinken aufgehört hast).

Dazu können gehören:

- Vermeide die Bar auf dem Nachhauseweg, indem du einen anderen Weg von der Arbeit nach Hause nimmst.
- Entferne dich aus den Gruppenchats deiner Freunde, indem du ihnen sagst, dass du zu deinem eigenen Wohlergehen eine Pause vom Ausgehen einlegst. (So vermeidest du auch, dass du dafür kritisiert wirst, dass du nicht ausgehst!)
- Vermeide es, die Dinge zu tun, die du immer tust, wenn du trinkst. Wenn du zum Beispiel zu Hause sitzt und trinkst, vermeide es, zu Hause zu sitzen. Geh spazieren. Lies ein Buch in einem anderen Raum. Geh ins Kino, zum

Bowling oder zu anderen Dingen, bei denen der Alkohol nicht im Mittelpunkt steht.

- Sage deiner Familie, dass du an einer Feier nicht teilnehmen kannst, weil du dir eine Auszeit für dein eigenes Wohlergehen nimmst. (Es kann sein, dass es dir der Familie gegenüber schwerer fällt, Grenzen zu setzen als bei Freunden – dennoch solltest du beides tun, wenn du erfolgreich nüchtern bleiben möchtest).

Wenn du die Maßnahmen aufschreibst, die du ergreifen solltest, wirst du oft feststellen, dass die, die am schwierigsten erscheinen, dich am schnellsten deinem Ziel näher bringen. Wenn du also die Motivation aufbringst, diese zuerst in Angriff zu nehmen, ist die Wahrscheinlichkeit groß, dass es sich auszahlt.

Top-Tipp: Du kennst dein Ziel – 24 Stunden lang nüchtern zu bleiben. Wann immer du mit etwas konfrontiert wirst, das dieses Ziel in Frage stellen könnte, z. B., wenn du mit Freunden auf einen Drink eingeladen bist, frage dich Folgendes:

Bringt mich mein Handeln meinem Ziel näher oder entfernt es mich davon?

Diese Frage gibt dir den Raum und die Zeit, darüber nachzudenken – mehr als du es getan hättest, wenn du auf Autopilot gewesen wärst.

So stimuliert dein Handeln deine Intuition

Das eigentliche Ziel beim Aufbau deiner Selbstwahrnehmung und beim Ergreifen positiver Maßnahmen ist das Training deiner Intuition. Das bedeutet, dass du ein Stadium erreichst, in dem dein Unterbewusstsein die *richtigen* Entscheidungen trifft. Es bedeutet, dass du die richtigen Gedanken und Gefühle hast und diese in die *richtigen* Handlungen einfließen.

Das ist das exakte Gegenteil von dem, was passiert, wenn du regelmäßig trinkst. Dann triffst du unbewusst schlechte Entscheidungen und bleibst in dem negativen Kreislauf.

Je mehr du an deiner Selbstwahrnehmung arbeitest, desto mehr wirst du in der Lage sein, positive Maßnahmen zu ergreifen und die damit verbundenen Vorteile zu spüren. Betrunkene Entscheidungen führen zu schrecklichen Ergebnissen – Verhaftungen wegen Trunkenheit am Steuer, Beziehungsabbrüche und abgelehnte Bankkartentransaktionen am Ende des Monats.

Intuitive, nüchterne Entscheidungen führen zu positiven und erfreulichen Ergebnissen – neue berufliche Chancen, gesunde neue Freundschaften und die Freude an nüchterner Kreativität.

Wenn dein Geist, dein Körper und deine Seele im Einklang sind, triffst du immer wieder die für dich richtigen Entscheidungen. Du verbesserst deine Intuition und dein „Bauchgefühl". (Wir werden in einem späteren Kapitel mehr über die Bauch-Hirn-Achse sprechen.)

Fehler passieren und sind Teil des Lernprozesses. Wenn du deine Intuition entwickelst, wirst du schnell merken, wenn du auf dem Weg Fehlentscheidungen triffst. Wenn das passiert, brauchst du dich nur noch an dein ZIEL zu erinnern. Dann überlegst du dir, welche positiven Maßnahmen du ergreifen kannst, um deinem Ziel näher zu kommen.

Fassen wir es noch einmal zusammen.

Es gibt drei Schritte, die du befolgen solltest, um das Ziel eines glücklichen und erfüllten nüchternen Lebens zu erreichen:

Die Entwicklung deiner Selbstwahrnehmung steht an erster Stelle, und damit hast du bereits begonnen. Es ist die Selbstwahrnehmung, die dich an den Punkt gebracht hat, an dem du erkannt hast, dass Alkohol dir nicht mehr gut tut.

Es gibt noch einiges zu tun, um die Selbstwahrnehmung zu verbessern. Es ist ein fortlaufender Prozess. Im vorigen Kapitel konntest du erfahren, dass es einige Werkzeuge gibt, die dir zur Verfügung stehen. Je mehr du verstehst, *warum* du trinkst, desto einfacher wird es, den nächsten Schritt konsequent zu gehen, nämlich:

Positive Maßnahmen ergreifen, dazu gehört, jeden Tag keinen Alkohol zu trinken. Wenn du das 24-Stunden-Ziel erreicht hast, fängst du am nächsten Tag erneut an und richtest deine Energie und deinen Fokus wieder darauf, nüchtern zu bleiben. Durch diesen Prozess des Handelns wirst du dir deiner selbst bewusster und entwickelst dich auf deinem Weg weiter.

Die Entwicklung deiner Intuition findet in gleichem Maße statt, wie sich dein Unterbewusstsein davon entfernt, „einen Drink" als Lösung für alles zu sehen. Stattdessen entwickelst du eine Intuition, die auf einem neuen, gesunden Autopiloten läuft, der bessere Entscheidungen trifft und bessere Ergebnisse erzielt..

Wenn du zum Beispiel anfängst, ein besseres Verständnis für deinen Geist, deinen Körper und deine Seele zu entwickeln, wirst du vielleicht Sport treiben und dich gesund ernähren, um eine stressige Woche auf der Arbeit zu bewältigen, anstatt den Stress mit einem Kater und fettigem Essen zu verstärken. Das sind zwei sehr unterschiedliche Möglichkeiten zu handeln, die zu zwei sehr unterschiedlichen Ergebnissen führen.

Über einen längeren Zeitraum betrachtet sind die Ergebnisse völlig unterschiedlich. Ich weiß das, denn ich habe sowohl die positiven als auch die negativen Kreisläufe erlebt.

Um nüchtern zu bleiben, ist es wichtig, sich überschaubare Ziele zu setzen (unter Verwendung der genannten SMART-Methodik). Der Traum von der Nüchternheit ist bedeutungslos ohne ein Ziel, das dir hilft, auf diesen Traum hinzuarbeiten.

Das zentrale Ziel, mit dem Trinken aufzuhören und nüchtern zu bleiben, bedeutet, dass ein

Rückfall zu keinem Zeitpunkt des Prozesses eine Katastrophe sein muss. Selbst wenn du einen Rückfall erleidest, entwickelst du deine Intuition weiter, solange du dich in deiner Selbstwahrnehmung übst und positive Maßnahmen ergreifst.

Die drei oben genannten Schritte zu lernen ist einfach, sie umzusetzen und durchzuhalten braucht jedoch Zeit, Geduld und Ausdauer.

Hier noch ein Tipp: Nimm dir jeden Morgen vor, „HEUTE nicht zu trinken". Mach dies zu deinem EINZIGEN Ziel zu Beginn der Nüchternheit und richte deine gesamte Energie und Konzentration darauf.

Indem du deine ganze Aufmerksamkeit zu Beginn eines jeden Tages auf dieses Ziel richtest, gibst du ihm die Anerkennung, die es verdient. Das wiederum wird dir helfen, den ganzen Tag über zu handeln.

Ich kann dir versichern, dass das tägliche Ziel „nicht zu trinken" mit der Zeit viel weniger Energie und Kraft von dir fordern wird. Sobald deine Selbstwahrnehmung und deine Intuition gestärkt sind, kannst du auch an all den anderen Dingen auf der Liste deiner Ziele arbeiten.

Als Nächstes betrachten wir die emotionale Intelligenz und wie die Arbeit daran deine Selbstwahrnehmung, deine Handlungen und deine Intuition verbessern kann.

Kapitel 3:

Das nüchterne Kind: Emotionale Intelligenz und wie du sie nutzen kannst

Emotionale Intelligenz ist die Fähigkeit, Emotionen zu erkennen, zu interpretieren und zu regulieren.

Es ist wichtig zu wissen, dass damit nicht nur die eigenen Emotionen gemeint sind. Bei echter emotionaler Intelligenz geht es auch um Empathie und darum, wie gut du die Gefühle deiner Mitmenschen verstehst.

Ein hohes Maß an emotionaler Intelligenz ist eine wünschenswerte Eigenschaft – in persönlichen Beziehungen und (zunehmend) auch am Arbeitsplatz. Es gibt viele Online-Tests, die deine emotionale Intelligenz „bewerten". Das

Ergebnis ist oft ein Emotionaler Quotient (EQ) – das Äquivalent des IQ für Intelligenz.

Deshalb ist emotionale Intelligenz der Schlüssel zu deiner Nüchternheit

Emotionale Intelligenz wirkt sich direkt auf unsere Selbstwahrnehmung und damit auch auf unser Handeln und unsere Intuition aus. Unsere Emotionen steuern unser Handeln. Je besser wir also unsere Emotionen *erkennen*, *interpretieren* und *regulieren* können, desto größer ist die Chance, dass wir die richtigen Maßnahmen ergreifen. Und das ist, wie wir festgestellt haben, ein entscheidender Schlüssel, um mit dem Trinken aufzuhören und nüchtern zu bleiben.

Um emotionale Intelligenz zu verstehen, ist es hilfreich, sich zunächst ein kleines Kind vorzustellen. Natürlich hat es nur eine begrenzte Auswahl an Grundemotionen, während es beginnt, die Welt um sich herum zu begreifen. In diesem Prozess empfindet es Emotionen, die ihm anfangs fremd sind. Mit der Zeit lernt es jedoch, seine Emotionen zu *erkennen*, zu *interpretieren* und zu *regulieren*, oder es lernt es nicht oder nicht richtig.

Ich habe noch keinen Erwachsenen gesehen, der im Supermarkt unkontrolliert geweint und einen Wutanfall bekommen hat. Das zeigt, dass wir auf einer gewissen Ebene alle emotional gereift sind, wenn wir erwachsen sind!

Es gibt eine Reihe von wissenschaftlichen Theorien darüber, wie viele Grundemotionen es gibt.[26] Der amerikanische Psychologe Paul Eckman zum Beispiel nennt sechs: Freude, Überraschung, Angst, Wut, Ekel, Trauer und Verachtung. Das Institut für Neurowissenschaften und Psychologie an der Universität Glasgow reduziert diese Liste auf nur vier und fasst Angst mit Überraschung und Wut mit Ekel zusammen.

Denken wir an das Kind zurück, so haben die Eltern schon nach kurzer Zeit die Möglichkeit, die Eckman'schen Grundemotionen bei ihren Sprösslingen zu erkennen. Sie lernen, Wut von Angst und Freude von Überraschung zu unterscheiden. Wahrscheinlich sehen sie, wie sich Ekel äußert, wenn sie dem Kind zum ersten Mal Brokkoli oder Blumenkohl füttern!

Wenn wir erwachsen werden, beginnen wir zu verstehen, dass es viele weitere komplexe und differenzierte Gefühle gibt, die über die sechs grundlegenden hinausgehen. „Glück" kann Stolz,

Begeisterung, Glückseligkeit, Zufriedenheit oder vieles mehr bedeuten. „Wut" kann ein Ausdruck von Frustration, Neid, Ohnmacht, Unbehagen oder Angst sein.

Nur weil wir verstehen, dass es Dutzende verschiedener Emotionen gibt, heißt das noch lange nicht, dass wir die emotionale Intelligenz entwickelt haben, sie zu erkennen – bei uns selbst oder bei anderen. Und solange wir sie nicht bei uns selbst erkennen, können wir sie auch nicht regulieren.

Damit sind wir beim eigentlichen Grund angelangt, warum die Verbesserung deiner emotionalen Intelligenz ein mächtiges Werkzeug ist, um deine Selbstwahrnehmung zu stärken und deine Ziele zu erreichen. Wenn du die Emotionen verstehst, die deine Handlungen steuern, ist es wahrscheinlicher, dass du in den positiven Kreisläufen bleibst, anstatt in die negativen zurückzufallen.

Zunächst sollten wir uns jedoch mit einem Problem befassen:

Alkohol ist *verheerend* für das emotionale Bewusstsein, denn viele Menschen sind darauf konditioniert, fast jeder Emotion mit Alkohol zu begegnen.

Wenn du wütend bist und dir angewöhnt hast, etwas zu trinken, um dich zu „beruhigen", bist du wahrscheinlich weit davon entfernt, herauszufinden, ob „wütend" tatsächlich Frustration, Neid, Ohnmacht, Unbehagen, Angst oder eine der vielen anderen komplexen Emotionen bedeutet.

Alkohol ist ein Betäubungsmittel, das uns daran hindert, unsere Emotionen wirklich wahrzunehmen und einen gesunden Weg zu finden, mit ihnen umzugehen. Eine Emotion taucht auf, und anstatt sie zuzulassen und zu verarbeiten, überschütten wir sie mit Alkohol. Und das gilt nicht nur für Alkohol – Menschen tun das oft auch mit Drogen, Essen, Sex, Glücksspiel und anderen Dingen.

Hast du schon einmal überflüssigerweise einen Snack gegessen, um das Gefühl der Langeweile zu vertreiben, oder online Sachen bestellt, die du gar nicht brauchst? Das sind Paradebeispiele dafür, wie man auch ohne Alkohol das Gefühl der Langeweile betäubt. Wenn du den Alkohol aufgibst und ihn gegen eine andere Sucht wie Shopping, Sex, Drogen, Beziehungen, Essen, Glücksspiel usw. eintauschst, kommt es häufig zu Kreuzabhängigkeiten.

Wenn du mit dem Trinken aufhörst, solltest du dir deiner Gewohnheiten bewusst werden und dich fragen: Befinde ich mich in dem gleichen Kreislauf von Suchtmittel > Bereuen > Wiederholen wie beim Alkohol? So kannst du mögliche Kreuzabhängigkeiten erkennen (bei mir persönlich war das Essen eine davon).

Diese Gewohnheit, jede unerwünschte Emotion zu verdrängen, wird von den Anonymen Alkoholikern mit den Worten „gereizt, ruhelos und unzufrieden" beschrieben. Der einzige Weg, dies zu überwinden, besteht im Erkennen unserer Emotionen und in der Entwicklung gesunder Wege, mit ihnen umzugehen.

Der Ausstieg aus dem Alkohol ist dabei nur der Anfang. Um Rückfälle zu vermeiden, sollten all diese Emotionen entwirrt und verarbeitet werden, wenn du nüchtern bist.

Wenn du das Gefühl hast, dass du bei einem EQ-Test nicht besonders gut abschneiden würdest, mach dir dafür keine Vorwürfe. Der Umfang deines emotionalen Vokabulars wurde vielleicht schon in deinen frühen Lebensjahren geprägt.

Zuvor haben wir uns damit befasst, dass viele Menschen leicht sagen würden, sie hätten eine "schöne Kindheit" genossen und die

Möglichkeit, dass sie in ihrer Kindheit ein Trauma erlebt haben, ausschließen.

Aber was wäre, wenn auf das Weinen Reaktionen wie „Reiß dich zusammen", „das reicht jetzt" oder „sei doch nicht so traurig" kämen? Was ist mit den Kindern, die bei Eltern aufwachsen, die selbst nie wirklich mehr als sechs einfache Emotionen entwickelt haben?

Nicht jedes Kind entwickelt die Fähigkeit, komplexe Gefühle zu benennen. Dieses Phänomen ist als Alexithymie bekannt. Tatsächlich ziehen emotional unreife Eltern emotional unreife Kinder auf, und ein Mangel an emotionaler Intelligenz lässt sich über Generationen nachvollziehen.

Mir fehlte es 17 Jahre lang an emotionaler Intelligenz – während meiner gesamten Trinkerkarriere. Der Alkohol machte mich emotional inkompetent und ich hatte keine Chance, an meinem EQ zu arbeiten.

Die gute Nachricht ist, dass wir in jedem Alter die Möglichkeit haben, unsere emotionale Intelligenz zu verbessern. Es ist sogar unerlässlich, das zu tun. Wenn wir nicht in der Lage sind, unsere wahren Emotionen zu erkennen und zu regulieren, ist es viel wahrscheinlicher, dass wir auf den großen roten „Sch**ß drauf"-Knopf drücken, wenn wir einer Emotion begegnen, mit der wir nicht umgehen können.

Und wie schaffen wir es, diesen Punkt zu überwinden?

Es gibt einen Grund, warum dieses Kapitel „Das nüchterne Kind" heißt.

Wenn Menschen auf Alkohol verzichten – manchmal zum ersten Mal seit Jahrzehnten – werden sie damit konfrontiert, sich mit all den Emotionen auseinanderzusetzen, die sie früher mit Alkohol verdrängt haben. Es kann sogar sein, dass es ihnen schwerfällt, diese Emotionen – abgesehen von der oben beschriebenen Grundauswahl – zu benennen, wenn es ihnen an der emotionalen Intelligenz fehlt.

Sie könnten sich zum Beispiel „wütend" fühlen, ohne zu wissen, dass sie eigentlich eifersüchtig sind.

Es ist durchaus möglich, dass du als erwachsene Person nie wirklich Gefühle erlebt hast, weil du immer Alkohol konsumiert hast, um zu vergessen und „Stress abzubauen". Wenn du dich Wochenende für Wochenende betäubst, wirst du zu einer Art Zombie – und nicht zu einem Menschen, der es mit der Welt aufnehmen und ihr seinen eigenen Stempel aufdrücken möchte.

Zu Beginn der Nüchternheit fühlen sich alle Emotionen sehr neu an. Das kann sich überwältigend und beängstigend anfühlen, wie der Zustand eines Kindes. Deshalb ist das Risiko eines Rückfalls hoch. Der Weg des geringsten Widerstands wäre die Rückkehr zu der einen Sache, die die Emotionen verschwinden lässt – Alkohol.

Deshalb ist es wichtig, dass du an deinen Emotionen arbeitest und lernst, sie zu lösen, ohne Alkohol zu trinken. Tust du das nicht, werden sie in Zukunft wieder auftauchen – möglicherweise mit katastrophalen Folgen.

Emotionale Intelligenz ist wichtig, denn sie ermöglicht es uns, das Leben mit weniger Stress, weniger emotionalen Reaktionen und mit weniger ungewollten Folgen zu meistern. Sie ist der Schlüssel, um negative Kreisläufe durch positive zu ersetzen.

Die Emotion „gereizt" ist eine, der du auf deinem Weg zu einem Leben ohne Alkohol sicher begegnen wirst. Es ist eine komplexe

Emotion, die unter nüchtern gewordenen Menschen oft diskutiert wird.

Sie tritt häufig auf, wenn ein regelmäßiger Wochenendtrinker das erste Mal einen Abend erlebt, zu dem er „Nein" sagen muss. Dann macht sich das große Gefühl von „FOMO" (Fear of Missing Out - Angst, etwas zu verpassen) breit.

Mit diesem Gefühl kommt die Gereiztheit, die manche als „die Weinhexe" oder „den Alkoholteufel" bezeichnen. Andere nennen es einfach „die Sucht".

Wenn du dieses Gefühl noch nie erlebt hast, wird es sich als extrem unangenehm bemerkbar machen. Du wirst dich so gelangweilt und wütend fühlen, als wäre das alles zutiefst ungerecht. Du wirst dir einreden, dass es nichts gibt, was du tun kannst, während deine Freunde unterwegs sind. (Das ist natürlich ein Irrglaube. Es gibt tausende von anderen Dingen, die du tun könntest).

Dein Gehirn wird dir dann einen Streich spielen und dich dazu bringen, zum ersten Drink zu greifen. Es wird dir Dinge sagen wie: „Einer wird schon gehen".

Es gibt einen ganz einfachen Weg, um das unangenehme Gefühl zu vertreiben.

Gib nach.

Geh raus.

Drücke den großen roten „Sch**ß drauf" -Knopf.

Das Problem ist, dass das nur zu einem Ergebnis führen kann. Du kommst direkt zurück in den negativen Kreislauf von trinken > verkatert sein > alles bereuen > eine Woche lang unglücklich sein.

Wenn du etwas anderes erreichen möchtest, MUSST du etwas anderes tun. Und das wird Emotionen hervorrufen, die dir nicht gefallen – anfangs. (Die gute Nachricht ist, dass es sich danach wahrscheinlich *nie wieder* so hart anfühlen wird wie beim ersten Mal.)

Du solltest es vermeiden, den „Sch**ß drauf"-Knopf zu drücken, denn das ist es, woran du arbeiten musst. Es WIRD sich unangenehm anfühlen. Du solltest dich daran gewöhnen, dich unwohl zu fühlen, denn nur so bleiben wir nüchtern und wachsen in allen Lebensbereichen.

Als du in die Schule gekommen bist, hast du das vielleicht auch als beängstigend empfunden.

Doch irgendwann, wenn du oft genug dort gewesen warst, war es nicht mehr so angsteinflößend. Es fühlte sich bald normal an.

So ist es auch mit der Nüchternheit: Am Anfang fühlt sie sich ungemütlich an, bis sie sich eines Tages normal anfühlt.

Dieses Gefühl der Gereiztheit musst du dir selbst bewusst machen. Du solltest es erkennen und lernen, welche *positiven Maßnahmen* du ergreifen kannst, um die Emotion, die es auslöst, zu *regulieren*, anstatt den großen roten Knopf zu drücken.

Das oben beschriebene Szenario ist eines, das mir immer wieder begegnet ist. Es brachte mich dazu, rückfällig zu werden – immer und immer wieder.

Ich hatte mit dem, was ich als „Langeweile" bezeichnete, wirklich zu kämpfen. Aber Langeweile ist kein Gefühl. Das *Gefühl* der Gereiztheit führt zu Langeweile (das ist der Glaube, dass es „nichts zu tun" gibt). Dieser Prozess gibt dem süchtigen Geist einen Grund, sich selbst zu sabotieren, und als Nächstes betrinkst du dich.

Was ist für mich jetzt anders?

Mit der Zeit habe ich gelernt, zu *erkennen*, wenn sich etwas nicht richtig anfühlt. Das *interpretiere* ich dann als das Gefühl der Reizbarkeit. Dann reguliere ich diese Emotion mit positiven Handlungen.

Je mehr du das tust und je mehr du deine Emotionen verstehst, desto mehr verbessert sich deine emotionale Intelligenz.

Anhand des obigen Beispiels, das wir „Freitagabend-FOMO" nennen, gibt es verschiedene Möglichkeiten, wie du die gereizte Emotion mit positiven Maßnahmen regulieren kannst.

Ich persönlich würde vielleicht ins Kino gehen oder einen Sportkurs für 20 Uhr buchen. Heute könnte ich vielleicht sogar für ein paar Stunden in die Kneipe gehen – aber mit einem soliden Ausstiegsplan und dem festen Vorsatz, nur alkoholfreie Getränke zu trinken. Ich kann *positiv* auf die Emotion der Gereiztheit reagieren, ohne zu trinken oder Drogen zu nehmen, und trotzdem früh schlafen gehen und am Samstagmorgen frisch aufwachen.

Bewegung ist ein wirksames Mittel, um deine Gefühle zu verändern. (Möglich, dass ich das schon öfter erwähnt habe!) Bewegung ist

Medizin, denn sie kann dich aus einer negativen Emotion herausholen und dir stattdessen eine positive geben.

Alkohol hingegen kann ein positives Gefühl (eine gute Woche im Job) in ein negatives verwandeln. Er kann dir ein stressiges Wochenende garantieren, weil du deprimiert bist, weil du einen lähmenden Kater hast und nichts erreicht hast.

Körperliche Aktivität kann die Emotionsregulierung verbessern. Sie senkt den Cortisolspiegel[27] der unsere Fähigkeit, klar zu denken, beeinträchtigt. Außerdem werden Wohlfühlstoffe (Endorphine und Dopamin) freigesetzt, die unser Gehirn in einen besseren Zustand versetzen, um unsere Gefühle zu regulieren.

Der Aufbau deiner emotionalen Intelligenz scheint ganz einfach zu sein, wenn es hier so geschrieben steht. Wenn du jedoch jahrelang Alkohol als Betäubungsmittel benutzt hast, kann es Jahre dauern, bis du das wieder voll und ganz in den Griff bekommst und dich wieder ausgeglichen fühlst.

So erkennst, interpretierst und regulierst du deine Emotionen

Hier erfährst du, wie du deine emotionale Intelligenz verbessern und deine Emotionen besser *erkennen, interpretieren* und *regulieren* kannst.

Phase 1: Erkennen von Emotionen

Zuerst solltest du daran arbeiten, deine Emotionen zu erkennen – was viel schwieriger ist, als viele Menschen denken. Denn wenn du nicht weißt, welche Emotion du fühlst, wie willst du dann lernen, sie zu deuten, geschweige denn, sie zu regulieren?

Emotionen können sich auf unterschiedlichste Weise äußern – sowohl mental als auch körperlich. Wut zum Beispiel kann sich anfühlen, als würde dein Blut kochen, und sie kann in Sekundenschnelle auftauchen. Sie kann von leichter Wut bis hin zu heftigem Zorn reichen. Wenn du Angst hast, kann dir übel werden, und wenn du glücklich bist, lächelst du.

Das folgende Rad der Emotionen zeigt eine Reihe von Grundemotionen sowie komplexere Emotionen, je weiter außerhalb, desto komplexer. Es unterstützt dich dabei,

Emotionen zu *erkennen*, damit du sie *interpretieren* kannst.

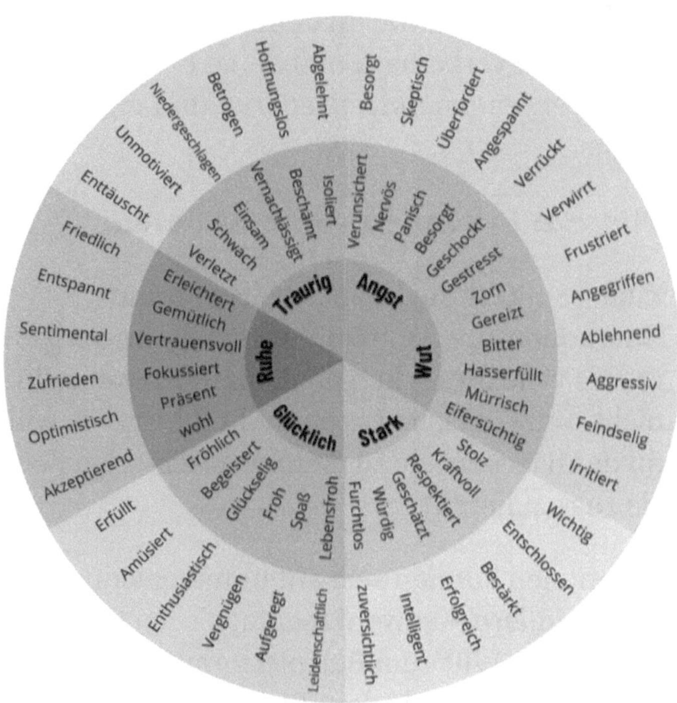

Wie bereits erwähnt, kann es sein, dass du nur die Grundemotionen in der Mitte erkennst, wenn deine emotionale Intelligenz in diesem Stadium nicht sehr ausgeprägt ist. Das Rad der Emotionen ist ein wirkungsvolles Werkzeug, mit dem du das überwinden kannst. Du fühlst zum Beispiel „Angst", aber in Wirklichkeit bist du vielleicht überwältigt, besorgt oder verunsichert.

Phase 2: Emotionen interpretieren

Wenn du die Emotion *erkannt* hast, die du gerade erlebst, kannst du sie *interpretieren*. Wie leicht dir das fällt, hängt von deiner emotionalen Intelligenz ab, und – ja – deine Kindheit spielt dabei auch eine Rolle.

Wenn du von Eltern mit einer hohen emotionalen Intelligenz großgezogen wurdest – Eltern, die ihre eigenen Emotionen verstanden und reguliert haben – wird diese Fähigkeit mit ziemlicher Sicherheit an dich weitergegeben worden sein.

Aber wenn in deiner Kindheit nur die Grundemotionen gezeigt, anerkannt und besprochen wurden, ist es keine Überraschung, dass du als Erwachsener Schwierigkeiten hast, Gefühle zu interpretieren. Wenn das Zeigen von Emotionen aktiv vermieden wurde – was sehr häufig der Fall ist –, wird dir dieser Prozess noch schwerer fallen.

Um zu *interpretieren*, was eine Emotion für dich bedeutet, ist es wichtig, dass du dich von deiner reaktiven Haltung zurückziehst. Stattdessen solltest du Raum schaffen, um die Emotion zu fühlen und nachzudenken, bevor du eine geeignete Maßnahme ergreifst, um mit ihr umzugehen. Mit den im Kapitel über Selbsterkenntnis erwähnten Werkzeugen kannst du dir diesen Raum schaffen, um sie zu interpretieren. Die Alternative wäre eine unüberlegte und unangemessene Handlung (z. B. die Entscheidung, zu trinken).

Sich mit den komplexeren Emotionen zu beschäftigen ist wirklich hilfreich. Wenn du erkennst, dass du tatsächlich frustriert, neidisch oder verbittert bist, kannst du damit viel besser arbeiten, als wenn du nur denkst, du wärst wütend.

Du wirst es nicht immer gleich gut hinbekommen. Manchmal interpretierst du eine Emotion falsch und ergreifst infolgedessen die falsche Maßnahme. Wenn du dich zum Beispiel nervös fühlst, kann das darauf hindeuten, dass dir etwas sehr am Herzen liegt, aber es ist möglich, dass du das mit Angst und Furcht verwechselst.

Sich zu irren, aus seinen Fehlern zu lernen und weiterzumachen, ist Teil des Prozesses. Unsere Emotionen sind oft vielschichtig, und es braucht Zeit, ihnen auf den Grund zu gehen. Eine Therapie und die Arbeit mit dem inneren Kind können dabei sehr hilfreich sein.

Phase 3: Emotionen rgulieren

Die dritte Phase ist der Schlüssel zur Verbesserung deiner emotionalen Intelligenz (und damit auch deines EQ-Wertes).

Emotionale Regulierung hat zwei ungesunde Extreme. Vielleicht erkennst du eines davon bei dir selbst. Du wirst sie *sicherlich* bei einigen Menschen, die du kennst, bemerken!

Am einen Ende der Skala befinden sich überreaktive Personen. Sie reagieren fast unmittelbar auf Dinge – oft mit Wut und Aggression. Es liegt keine Zeit zwischen dem Empfinden einer Emotion und der Reaktion darauf – oft auf eine ungesunde oder irrationale Weise.

Am anderen Ende des Spektrums befinden sich Personen, die sich emotional abkapseln. Ironischerweise sind das manchmal Menschen, die Emotionen erkennen und interpretieren KÖNNEN – aber nicht in der Lage sind, sie zu regulieren.

Emotionales Abschalten mag für manche Menschen erstrebenswerter erscheinen als über die Stränge zu schlagen. Es gibt sogar Leute (und einige Kulturen), die das befürworten, doch es ist ungesund und eine Form der Selbstsabotage.

Stell dir zum Beispiel vor, ein Freund leiht sich ständig Geld von dir und zahlt es nicht zurück. Wenn du überreagierst, könntest du die Tür eintreten und die Nerven verlieren. Wahrscheinlich ist das nicht das Beste, was du tun kannst.

Emotional abzuschalten könnte bedeuten, nichts zu sagen. Das führt dazu, dass du das Problem in Gedanken wiederholst, die Situation nicht löst und wichtige Tagesenergie verbrauchst, die du für produktivere Dinge verwenden könntest. Außerdem würdest du diesem Freund ungewollt signalisieren, dass er oder sie dich weiterhin inakzeptabel behandeln kann.

Wenn du dich emotional abkapselst, lebst du weiter mit den Gefühlen und den negativen Folgen, die entstehen, wenn du dich nicht mit ihnen auseinandersetzt. Das ist anstrengend.

Zum Glück gibt es einen gesunden Mittelweg auf der Skala der Emotionsregulierung: Schaffe dir Raum, um zu fühlen und nachzudenken, bevor du auf angemessene Weise handelst. Das kann bedeuten, dass du ruhig, aber bestimmt deinen Standpunkt darlegst – und dann noch einmal überlegst, was du tun solltest, wenn du die Antwort deines Freundes hörst.

Hier ist ein persönliches Beispiel dafür, wie emotionale Intelligenz in der Praxis funktioniert und dabei alle drei Phasen durchläuft: *Erkennen, Interpretieren* und *Regulieren* von Emotionen.

Früher habe ich am Donnerstagabend nach der Arbeit (viel) getrunken. Heute weiß ich, dass das vor allem daran lag, dass ich in meinem Job sehr unglücklich war.

Leider verdeckte das Trinken (und die daraus resultierenden Kater) das Gefühl des Unglücklichseins. Es dauerte Jahre, bis ich es *erkannte*. Erst nach einem Jahr Nüchternheit war ich in der Lage zu erkennen, wie unglücklich und unerfüllt ich mich in meinem Job fühlte.

Um zu *verstehen,* warum ich unglücklich war, war es notwendig den Prozess zu durchlaufen. Ich war nüchtern und ich hatte einen Job, der gut bezahlt wurde. Zudem hatte ich wieder eine tolle Beziehung zu meiner Familie. Außenstehend hätten die meisten angenommen, dass es mir gut geht.

Trotzdem war die vorherrschende Emotion, die ich an jedem einzelnen Arbeitstag empfand, Unzufriedenheit. Schließlich akzeptierte ich, dass der Job mich trotz des Geldes und der Sicherheit, die er mir bot, unglücklich machte.

Als ich nüchtern wurde, konnte ich mich besser auf meine Gefühle einstellen. Ich merkte, dass ich mein Leben selbst in der Hand hatte statt auf dem Beifahrersitz zu sitzen. (Emotionen zu deuten war sehr neu, aber auch sehr bestärkend für mich).

Nachdem ich *erkannt* hatte, dass ich in meinem Job unglücklich war und *herausgefunden* hatte, dass das daran lag, dass die Arbeit, die ich tat, nicht mit meinem neuen, nüchternen Selbst in Einklang stand, war ich bereit für die letzte Phase: die *Regulierung* dieser Emotion des Unglücklichseins.

Schockierenderweise brauchte ich insgesamt 12 JAHRE, um an diesen Punkt zu gelangen! Die ganze Zeit über hatte der Alkohol meine Gefühle betäubt!

Ich war endlich in der Lage, die richtigen, positiven Maßnahmen zu ergreifen, indem ich mir einen Job suchte, der zu dem passte, was ich war und wo ich hin wollte.

Das erscheint jetzt alles ziemlich einfach. Aber Millionen von Menschen stecken jahrelang, wenn nicht sogar ein Leben lang, in einem unglücklichen Kreislauf fest, weil sie nicht in der Lage sind, ihre Emotionen zu *erkennen*, zu *interpretieren* und zu *regulieren*.

Emotionale Intelligenz hat einen enormen Einfluss. Du kannst sie auf jedes Gefühl anwenden, das dir im Laufe deines Lebens begegnet. Je mehr du das tust, desto mehr entwickelst du deine Intuition und triffst immer wieder die richtigen Entscheidungen – für dich und deine Zukunft.

Um nüchtern zu bleiben ist es wichtig, dass du deine Emotionen verstehst, damit du nicht mit Alkohol darauf reagierst. Stattdessen regulierst du sie und reagierst mit sicheren Alternativen, die dir helfen, das Trinken ganz zu vermeiden.

Im nächsten Kapitel geht es darum, das Verlangen und die Trigger zu verstehen. Auch hier ist emotionale Intelligenz der Schlüssel, um uns klar zu machen, was uns emotional zu einem Rückfall verleiten kann.

Sei nicht überrascht, wenn es dir nicht leicht fällt, Emotionen zu *erkennen*, zu *interpretieren* und zu *regulieren*. Leider ist das Unvermögen dazu bei Menschen, die sich daran gewöhnt haben, Alkohol als Bewältigungsmechanismus zu nutzen, sehr verbreitet.

Wenn das auf dich zutrifft, könnte ein Therapeut oder eine Therapeutin eine große Hilfe sein. Sie unterstützen dich dabei, deine Emotionen zu verstehen und auf eine gesündere und positivere Weise auf sie zu reagieren.

Wenn du dich festgefahren fühlst und Schwierigkeiten hast, Emotionen wie Wut oder Traurigkeit zu überwinden, ohne zum Alkohol zu greifen, könnte es der richtige Zeitpunkt sein, um professionelle Hilfe in Anspruch zu nehmen.

Eine therapeutische Fachkraft kann dir eine Art Spiegel vorhalten, dir wirkungsvolle Fragen stellen und dir dabei helfen, eine tiefere Ebene der Selbstwahrnehmung zu erreichen, die dir allein vielleicht nicht zugänglich ist.

Egal, ob du deine emotionale Intelligenz mit Therapie oder im Alleingang verbesserst, mit der Zeit wirst du merken, wie du dich veränderst. Du wirst beginnen, deine Emotionen zu erkennen, zu sehen, wie sich dein Verhalten entwickelt und wie es sich auf dein intuitives Handeln auswirkt.

Dann wirst du anfangen, dich konsequent für die positiven Kreisläufe, die dir gut tun, zu entscheiden.

Groll und die Kunst des Loslassens

„Groll ist wie Gift zu trinken und darauf zu warten, dass die andere Person stirbt". Malachy McCourt.[28]

Es lohnt sich, etwas genauer auf den Groll einzugehen. Er spielt auch innerhalb des Zwölf-Schritte-Programm der Anonymen Alkoholiker eine wichtige Rolle. Es ist nicht zu übersehen, wie stark das Zwölf-Schritte-Programm verbitterte, verdrehte Alkoholiker in versöhnliche, liebevolle, fürsorgliche und nüchterne Vorbilder verwandelt hat.

Es nicht nötig, die Anonymen Alkoholiker zu mögen, um zu erkennen, dass was sie tun, schon seit langem funktioniert. Die Überwindung von Groll und Verbitterung ist der Schlüssel zum Erfolg.

Verbitterung bewirkt zwei Dinge:

1. Es hindert dich daran, ganz im Jetzt sein, da du ständig an die vergangenen Situationen denkst, die den Groll

verursacht haben (zum Beispiel, dass du bei der Arbeit nicht befördert wurdest).

2. Es verbraucht eine Menge Energie. Du denkst ständig über den Groll nach und zermürbst dich selbst, was auch körperlichen Stress verursacht.

Wenn du lernst, deinen Groll zu überwinden, kannst du bei deinen täglichen Aktivitäten voll präsent sein. Das bedeutet auch, dass du deine Lebensenergie nicht für Situationen vergeudest, über die du keine Kontrolle hast.

Den Groll loszulassen ist eine Kunstform. Es braucht seine Zeit, aber du lernst schnell, dass dich das Festhalten am Groll im Leben nicht weiterbringt. Stattdessen hält es dich in einer negativen Vergangenheit fest, die du nicht kontrollieren kannst.

Als ich mit dem Trinken aufgehört habe, hasste ich alle. Ich hasste die Tatsache, dass sie alle im Leben weiter waren. Ich löschte meine Profile in den sozialen Medien, weil ich es hasste, Menschen glücklich zu sehen. Alles erinnerte mich daran, wie besch*ssen ich mich fühlte.

Ich ärgerte mich über jeden und alles, weil ich so unglücklich über mein eigenes Leben war. Alkohol und andere Drogen fühlten sich wie die einzige vorübergehende Lösung für dieses Gefühl an, auch wenn ich damit schon bald auf dem Weg zum Entzug war.

Diese Kreisläufe sind extrem toxisch – und sie werden zu einer sich selbst erfüllenden Prophezeiung. Ich *dachte*, ich sei *wertlos*, also *wurde* ich *wertlos*. Das alles wurde durch meinen Groll vorangetrieben und brachte mich dazu, zu trinken. Es war extrem schwierig, diesen Kreislauf zu durchbrechen, bis ich nüchtern wurde und anfing, daran zu arbeiten (der vierte Schritt im Zwölf-Schritte-Programm).

Groll ist ein starkes Gefühl, das zu einem Rückfall führt, weil der Alkohol uns unglaublich kurzzeitig das Gefühl gibt, „schlecht behandelt" zu werden. Ich habe lange Zeit in diesem Kreislauf festgesteckt. Deshalb war das Verstehen von Groll und Verbitterung ein wichtiger Teil meines Weges.

Wenn du anfängst, auf Papier zu notieren, wen und was du verachtest, wirst du schnell ein Muster erkennen: Der Alkohol bringt dich gegen die Welt auf! Du lebst in einem unheimlich tragischem Mindset, wenn du alles und jeden hasst. (Ich bin mir sicher, dass du das auch bei anderen Menschen beobachtet hast, die sich über alles beschweren und jammern!)

Im Folgenden findest du eine Tabelle, die du kopieren und in die du deine Ressentiments eintragen kannst. Schreibe auf, wer oder was dich stört, warum dich diese Person oder diese Sache stört, welche Emotionen das auslöst und inwiefern du glaubst, wie es dir weiterhelfen könnte, wenn du ihn loslässt.

Nimm dir Zeit – bei den Anonymen Alkoholikern kann es Jahre dauern, bis eine Person diesen Schritt abschließt und zum nächsten übergeht, weil sie im Laufe der Jahre viele Menschen und Orte angesammelt hat, auf die sie einen Groll hegt. Das ist eine außerordentlich therapeutische Übung – vor allem, wenn du eine Menge unnötigen Ballast mit dir herumgetragen hast.

Auf wen oder was hast du einen Groll?	Was war die Ursache für den Groll?	Welche Gefühle löst das bei dir aus? (Benutze das Rad.)	Was erreichst du, wenn du den Groll loslässt?
Wendy	Sie wurde auf der Arbeit vor mir befördert.	Ungerecht behandelt und traurig.	Ich kann nach vorne blicken, um Feedback bitten, warum ich den Job nicht bekommen habe, und mich bei der nächsten

			Gelegenheit verbessern.
Tommy	Ihm geht es wirklich gut – ein schönes Auto, ein schönes Haus, eine hinreißende Freundin.	Angst, dass ich nicht gut genug bin.	Ich kann mich auf mein eigenes Leben konzentrieren – mir Sorgen darüber zu machen, wo andere im Leben stehen, hilft mir nicht, in meinem Leben weiterzukommen.

Übrigens kannst du immer wieder eine neue Liste erstellen – auch wenn du nüchtern bist. Seit ich mit dem Trinken aufgehört habe, empfinde ich immer noch Ressentiments gegenüber Menschen. Es kommt und geht, aber der Unterschied besteht darin, dass ich es erkenne, interpretiere, was es für mich bedeutet, und es dann loslassen kann. Oft spiegelt es wider, wie ich mich fühle (verängstigt, wütend, traurig usw.), und nicht, was die Person tatsächlich getan hat.

Normalerweise hat die Person, über die du dich ärgerst, keine Ahnung, wie viel Zeit und Energie du damit verschwendest, dich über sie zu ärgern! Sie wird wahrscheinlich nicht einmal wissen, dass es überhaupt ein Problem gibt!

Die Überwindung deines Grolls ist ein wichtiger Schritt, um dich von Dingen zu befreien, über die du keine Kontrolle hast (wie andere Menschen, Orte oder Dinge). Das gibt dir die Möglichkeit, eine der stärksten Emotionen, die einen Rückfall verursachen, zu kontrollieren, ohne zur Flasche zu greifen.

Sobald du dir deines Grolls bewusst geworden bist, kannst du positive Maßnahmen ergreifen, um zu verhindern, dass er sich auf deine Abstinenz auswirkt. Mit der Zeit wirst du eine Intuition entwickeln, die diese Aufgabe erleichtert.

Zeichen deiner emotionale Reife

Es ist schön und gut, diese Übungen zu machen, aber wie wir bereits unter dem Punkt „Messbar" bei den SMART-Zielen erwähnt haben: Wenn du es nicht messen kannst, kannst du es auch nicht verbessern.

Du kannst online einen Test zur emotionalen Intelligenz machen und deine Ergebnisse im Laufe der Zeit vergleichen. Oder du nimmst dir die Zeit, anhand der folgenden Punkte zu reflektieren, ob du emotional reifer wirst (oder nicht):

- Du verstehst, dass manche Menschen nur negative Verhaltensweisen an den Tag legen und erkennst, dass du dich ihnen nicht auf diesem selbstzerstörerischen Weg anschließen musst. Das könnte bedeuten, dass du zu dem Treffen am Freitagabend „Nein" sagst.

- Du bist dafür verantwortlich, wie du auf deine Mitmenschen reagierst und lernst, deine Gefühle zu regulieren. Wenn deine Freunde dich zum Beispiel zu „nur einem Drink" überreden wollen, bleibst du lieber zu Hause, statt auf den großen roten Knopf zu drücken.

- Du verstehst, dass Menschen ihre eigenen Entscheidungen über ihr Leben treffen. Du verstehst, dass es nicht deine Aufgabe ist, Menschen zu ändern oder zu kontrollieren oder anderen deine Überzeugungen aufzuzwingen.

- Wenn du nüchtern wirst und die vielen Vorteile genießt, möchtest du der Welt erzählen, wie toll es ist, aber dann begreifst du schnell, dass du Menschen nicht zwingen kannst, sich zu ändern – sie müssen es selbst wollen. Dieses Buch gibt dir Anleitungen, die dir helfen, dich zu ändern. Es liegt ganz bei dir, ob du sie nutzt oder nicht.

- Du kannst Meinungsverschiedenheiten tolerieren. (Das trägt auch dazu bei, das Ego anderer Menschen zu schmälern – dazu später mehr). Es ist gesund, anderer Meinung zu sein – du musst nicht blind folgen und schon gar nicht zulassen, dass Meinungsverschiedenheiten den Rest deines Tages/Woche/Monats/Jahres ruinieren.
- Du schaffst dir Raum und Zeit, um zu reagieren, indem du die Dinge durchdenkst und fundierte Entscheidungen triffst, anstatt nur zu reagieren.
- Du lernst, gesunde emotionale Grenzen zu setzen und kannst „Nein" sagen, ohne dich schuldig zu fühlen oder Angst davor zu haben, was andere denken könnten. Du hörst auf, es anderen recht zu machen und stellst deine Nüchternheit über alle anderen an die erste Stelle.
- Du kannst Dinge loslassen, die dich dazu gebracht hätten, zum Alkohol zu greifen. Das ist echte Reife.

Wenn du anfängst, einige dieser Punkte in deinem Alltag zu sehen, bist du auf dem besten Weg, deine emotionale Intelligenz zu verbessern!

***

Welche Emotion empfindest du, wenn du beschließt, den großen roten „Sch**ß drauf"-Knopf zu drücken und nach einem Drink zu greifen?

Das obige Rad der Emotionen hilft dir, das zu ermitteln. Wenn du herausgefunden hast, wie du dich fühlst, nimm dir etwas Zeit, um herauszufinden, warum dieses Gefühl bei dir auftaucht.

Die Verarbeitung deiner Gefühle ist keine exakte Wissenschaft. Die Umstände werden sich selten wiederholen. Es geht jedoch darum, dass du dich bewusst mit deinen Emotionen auseinandersetzt und herausfindest, was dich zum Trinken verleitet. Und damit sind wir auch schon beim nächsten Kapitel.

KAPITEL 4:

MENSCHEN, ORTE UND DINGE: DAS VERLANGEN UND DIE TRIGGER VERSTEHEN – UND DAMIT UMGEHEN

Manchmal ist es relativ einfach, nicht zu trinken. In anderen Situationen ist es umso schwieriger.

Wenn du schon länger trinkst und das Verlangen nach Alkohol verspürst, ist das ganz natürlich. Die wissenschaftliche Erklärung, wie Alkohol auf das Gehirn wirkt, macht deutlich, warum.

Alkohol überflutet die Belohnungsschaltkreise des Gehirns mit Dopamin[29], , das oft als „Wohlfühl"-Neurotransmitter bezeichnet wird. (Es ist erwähnenswert, dass viele andere Dinge deinen Dopaminspiegel ansteigen lassen: Sport, Sex, Essen, das Erreichen von Zielen, Einkaufen oder alles andere, was dir Spaß macht. Die meisten dieser Dinge sind viel besser für dich als Alkohol!)

Das Problem besteht darin, dass Alkohol mit der Zeit deinen natürlichen Dopaminspiegel senkt. Infolgedessen passt sich das Gehirn an die unnatürliche Dopaminflut an und produziert weniger Dopamin.

Wenn weniger Dopamin vorhanden ist, wenn du nicht trinkst, hast du das Verlangen nach mehr Alkohol – weil du glaubst, dass du dich dann besser fühlst.

Trigger sind etwas anderes als das Verlangen, aber sie sind eng miteinander verbunden. Tatsächlich sind Trigger die Ausöser, die zu Verlangen *führen*.

Trigger gibt es in allen Formen und Farben: in der Nähe von bestimmten Menschen, in bestimmten Umgebungen und bei alltäglichen Belastungen und Stress. Sogar ein bestimmter Geruch (auch wenn er nichts mit Alkohol zu tun hat) kann ein Trigger sein.

Hier ist ein typisches Beispiel: 16:00 Uhr an einem Freitag kann eine triggernde Zeit sein, um über Alkohol nachzudenken. Vielleicht fangen alle an, darüber zu reden, in welche Bar sie nach der Arbeit gehen wollen. Dieser Trigger führt dann zu einem Verlangen. Das „Freitagsgefühl", von dem viele Leute berichten, ist nichts anderes als ein Verlangen nach Alkohol – ausgelöst durch die einfache Tatsache, dass es Freitag ist!

Das kann zu körperlicher Reizbarkeit und geistiger Frustration führen: Du willst einen Drink, aber du willst auch nüchtern bleiben.

Das ist der Zeitpunkt, an dem du an das denkst, was du in den vorherigen Kapiteln gelernt hast: Es ist wichtig, dass du dir deiner Trigger und deines Verlangens **bewusst** wirst, damit du in der Lage bist, **positive Maßnahmen** zu ergreifen, um einen Rückfall zu vermeiden. Je mehr du dies erfolgreich tust, desto mehr entwickelst du deine Intuition und vertraust deinem Unterbewusstsein, diese Entscheidungen für dich zu treffen.

Noch einmal: Es ist ein positiver Kreislauf im Gegensatz zu einem negativen Kreislauf. Die Alternative wäre: Trinken > Bereuen > Wiederholen …

Es gibt noch eine weitere wichtige Erkenntnis über das Verlangen, Trigger, Dopamin und die Sucht. Eine wissenschaftliche Studie über die Mechanismen eines Rückfalls bestätigt, dass

„die Wiederaufnahme des Drogenkonsums nach der Abstinenz vor dem Kontakt mit der Droge selbst stattfindet und durch Umweltreize, Gedanken oder Stressfaktoren ausgelöst wird."[30]

Drogensüchtige sagen oft, dass die Jagd nach Drogen und das Ritual ihrer Zubereitung genauso viel Rausch erzeugt wie die Einnahme der Drogen selbst. Eine Parallele für Trinkende ist die Planung des Abends, die Entscheidung, wohin sie gehen möchten und die Vorbereitung.

Die Wissenschaft unterstützt dies. Eine Studie zeigt, dass die Ausschüttung von Dopamin allein durch die Erwartung, eine Substanz zu konsumieren, *ausgelöst* werden kann.[31] Das mag zwar unnötig erscheinen, ist aber sehr nützlich, wenn es darum geht, deine Auslöser zu erkennen.

Im Laufe der Zeit hat dein Gehirn starke neuronale Verknüpfungen zum Alkoholkonsum (und möglicherweise auch zu anderen Drogen) aufgebaut. Es ist wichtig, dass du daran arbeitest, diese starken Verbindungen zwischen Alkoholkonsum und verschiedenen Menschen, Orten und Dingen zu beseitigen.

Das Dopamin, das dein Verlangen antreibt, wird ausgeschüttet, noch bevor du den ersten Schluck trinkst. Das Ziel ist also, die Menschen, Orte und Dinge zu meiden, die stark mit dem Trinken verbunden sind.

Wie bei der Erziehung eines Welpen musst du neue Verhaltensweisen positiv verstärken – das ist besonders in den ersten Tagen wichtig.

Schauen wir uns ein paar häufige Trigger an, die du dir selbst bewusst machen solltest.

Menschen (Freunde, Familie und Kollegen)

Niemand behauptet, dass du, wenn du nüchtern bist, allen Leuten aus dem Weg gehen sollst, mit denen du jemals etwas getrunken hast. Aber deine trinkenden (oder drogennehmenden) Freunde sind unweigerlich gefährliche Trigger für dich. Oft haben Gruppen von Trinkern und/oder Drogenkonsumenten einen gemeinsamen Mangel an Selbstbewusstsein und emotionaler Reife.

Es führt kein Weg daran vorbei: Wenn du viel Zeit mit Leuten verbringst, mit denen du dich schon oft betrunken hast, ist die Gefahr eines Rückfalls besonders groß.

Wenn du ernsthaft mit dem Trinken aufhören möchtest, ist ein gutes Mantra, das du dir merken solltest: „Die Freunde, die es stört, sind unwichtig, und die Freunde, die es nicht stört, sind wichtig."

Du wirst besser als alle anderen wissen, welche Menschen in deinem Leben die lästigsten Trigger sind, wenn du keinen Alkohol trinken möchtest. Bei mir waren meine Trink- und Drogenkumpel ein großes Problem, aber es können auch bestimmte Arbeitskollegen, Familienmitglieder, deine Fußballmannschaft oder die Müttergruppe in der Schule sein.

Grenzen sind wichtig und für Familienmitglieder genauso wichtig wie für Freunde und Kollegen. Auch wenn es dir vielleicht schwerer fällt „Nein" zu Familienmitgliedern zu sagen, sollte deine Nüchternheit über allen anderen stehen – auch über deiner Familie.

Wahrscheinlich musst du in den ersten Tagen extremer vorgehen, um Trigger zu vermeiden, als du es nach einiger Zeit der Nüchternheit tun wirst. Es wird etwas dauern, bis sich neue Gewohnheiten herausbilden und neue Nervenbahnen entstehen, also sind Geduld und Ausdauer gefragt. Das könnte bedeuten, dass du kurzfristig auf gesellschaftliche Veranstaltungen verzichten musst. (Das wird dir schnell helfen, herauszufinden, welche Freunde dich stören und welche Freunde wichtig sind!)

Es ist auch erstaunlich einfach, über soziale Netzwerke und persönliche Gruppen neue „nüchterne Freunde" zu finden. Die Tatsache, dass Nüchternheit ein immer beliebterer Trend ist, bedeutet, dass es viele Gleichgesinnte gibt.

Wenn du dich entschließt, dich wieder in Szenen zu begeben, in denen viel getrunken wird, sind Pläne und Strategien wichtig. Ein nüchterner Kumpel oder ein bester Freund könnte dich zur Rechenschaft ziehen (obwohl letzteres eine Herausforderung sein kann, wenn deine Gruppe gerne trinkt).

Die Visualisierung und Planung im Voraus hilft dir, deine Angst vor der Teilnahme an einer Veranstaltung mit Alkohol abzubauen. Wenn du dir vorher überlegst, welche alkoholfreien Getränke es gibt, fühlst du dich nicht unter Druck gesetzt, wenn du an der Bar stehst und bereits nervös bist. „Wer nicht plant, plant zu scheitern" ist ein guter Spruch, den du dir merken solltest, wenn du nüchterne Nächte an Orten planst, an denen du weißt, dass Alkohol fließen wird.

Plane eine Ausstiegsstrategie, überlege dir, welche alkoholfreien Getränke du genießen kannst, und sei bereit, Grenzen zu setzen. Sag „Nein" und lass dich nicht beschimpfen.

Menschen, die Dinge sagen wie „Ach, komm schon" und „Warum bist du so langweilig?", sind nicht die Art von Menschen, die du um dich haben willst, wenn du dein Leben positiv veränderst. Bedenke, dass du das für dein eigenes Wohlbefinden tust.

Nüchternheit ist dein einziges Ziel – also gib anderen Menschen nicht die Macht, es zu zerstören.

Orte (Kneipen, Clubs, Feiertage, Sportstätten, Beerdigungen, Hochzeiten und mehr!)

Wie oben erklärt, stellt dein Gehirn im Laufe der Zeit starke neuronale Belohnungsverknüpfungen zu deinen Gewohnheiten her. Wenn du zum Beispiel einen Ort besuchst, den du stark mit Alkohol assoziierst, wird dein Gehirn wahrscheinlich Dopamin ausschütten und dich zu einem starken Verlangen nach Alkohol führen.

Wenn du etwas anderes möchtest, solltest du die Dinge anders angehen. Um ein neues alkoholfreies Leben zu beginnen, solltest du mit der Gewohnheit brechen, du selbst zu sein.

Ich habe zum Beispiel früher in einer Kneipe getrunken, in der ich gearbeitet und gewohnt habe. Außerdem kaufte ich in dieser Kneipe Drogen, und ich fuhr fast immer an ihr vorbei.

Sechs Monate lang bin ich nicht dort vorbeigefahren – auch wenn jede Fahrt zusätzliche Zeit kostete. Ich musste diese Verbindung unterbrechen und mein Gehirn neu vernetzen, um ein neues, nüchternes Leben zu führen.

Ich fahre immer noch gelegentlich an der Kneipe vorbei, und meine Gedanken kreisen immer noch um Alkohol und Drogen. Der Unterschied ist, dass ich nicht mehr auf diese Gedanken reagiere. Die Verbindung zur Belohnung ist nicht mehr da.

Wie kannst du mit Triggern umgehen, die mit Orten verbunden sind?

Nimm andere Routen und meide die Kneipen, in denen du früher getrunken hast (zumindest in der Anfangszeit). Sei dir bewusst, dass du dich bewusst darum bemühst, dein Gehirn neu zu programmieren. Das wird dazu beitragen, die starken Assoziationen zu schwächen, die du mit Alkohol aufgebaut hast. Und die können wirklich stark sein – sie wurden über Jahre oder sogar Jahrzehnte hinweg aufgebaut.

Finde neue Orte, an denen du Zeit verbringen kannst. Schlage deinen Freunden vor, dich in einem Café zu treffen, nicht in einer Kneipe. Wenn sie „Nein" sagen, ist es vielleicht an der Zeit, sich neue Freunde zu suchen!

Das Wichtigste ist, neue Orte zu finden, die nicht mit deinen alten Verhaltensmustern in Verbindung gebracht werden. Die gute Nachricht ist, dass es davon jede Menge gibt. Sobald du nicht mehr gezwungen bist, nur Orte zu wählen, an denen Alkohol ausgeschenkt wird, merkst du schnell, wie viele andere Alternativen es gibt.

Dinge (Buchstäblich ALLES)

Der Umgang mit Triggern in der Nähe von Menschen und Orten ist schon schwierig genug. Leider gibt es noch viele weitere Dinge, die diese lästigen Neuronen in Wallung bringen können, wie Gerüche, Zeiten, Geschmäcker und Aktivitäten.

Für manche Ex-Trinkende sind der Geruch und der Geschmack von alkoholfreiem Bier ein zu großer Auslöser (obwohl es erwähnenswert ist, dass es für viele einfacher ist, wenn es eine große Auswahl an alkoholfreien Getränken gibt. Nur du wirst wissen, wie es bei dir aussieht).

Utensilien können triggern: Zigaretten, Biergläser, Weingläser, Bierdeckel - sogar Geldscheine für Kokainkonsumenten!

In den Urlaub zu fahren ist oft ein großer Auslöser. Selbst das Buchen eines Urlaubs kann ein Auslöser sein. Die Assoziation von Entspannung und Vergnügen kann ausreichen, um das Dopamin zum Fließen zu bringen und dich dazu zu bringen, eine Flasche Wein zum Feiern aufzumachen.

Viele nüchterne Menschen tun sich besonders schwer damit, ihre erste Hochzeit zu besuchen. Die Assoziation zwischen Hochzeiten und exzessivem Trinken ist unglaublich ausgeprägt!

Ich habe mit Ex-Trinkenden gesprochen, die durch Grillpartys, Sonnenschein und bestimmte Lieder ausgelöst werden. Vielleicht kannst du jetzt noch nicht alle deine Trigger aufzählen, aber du kannst dir sicher sein, dass du sie mit der Zeit herausfinden wirst!

Dieser Prozess der Neuvernetzung braucht Zeit. Manchmal fühlt es sich leicht, lohnend und beglückend an. Viele Menschen erleben in den ersten Tagen des Verzichts die „nüchternen Flitterwochen" oder fühlen sich, als ob sie auf einer „rosa Wolke" schweben würden.

Aber lass dich nicht täuschen. Unterbewusste Konditionierungen können tiefgreifend sein, und selbst nach Jahren kannst du feststellen, dass etwas Banales ein Verlangen auslöst.

So gehst du mit Triggern um

In den ersten Tagen ist die einfachste Art, mit Triggern umzugehen, „Nein" zu den Dingen zu sagen, von denen du weißt, dass sie eine Herausforderung darstellen.

Sobald du eine gewisse Zeit nüchtern bist und an deiner Selbstwahrnehmung gearbeitet hast, wirst du dich wieder an gesellschaftliche Veranstaltungen und andere Dinge herantasten, die du als trinkende Person unternommen hast. Du wirst vielleicht feststellen, dass du sie sogar noch mehr genießen kannst, besonders Sport und Hobbys.

Ein weiterer wichtiger Punkt ist, dass Stress oft der größte Trigger ist.

Natürlich hast du keine volle Kontrolle über die stressigen Situationen, denen du begegnest. Aber du kannst lebensverändernde Ereignisse vermeiden, die deinen Stresspegel mit Sicherheit erhöhen. Wenn du zum Beispiel dabei bist, mit dem Trinken aufzuhören, ist es wahrscheinlich nicht der beste Zeitpunkt, umzuziehen, einen Welpen zu bekommen (glaub mir) oder den Job zu wechseln.

Stress in kleinen Dosen ist jedoch gesund. Nur wenn wir stressige Situationen durchleben, können wir etwas über uns selbst lernen und uns in Zukunft besser gegen solche Situationen wappnen. In den ersten Tagen geht es also darum, den Stress in kleinen Schritten zu bewältigen und nicht gleich alles auf eine Karte zu setzen. Ich habe an vielen AA-Meetings und Gruppentherapiesitzungen teilgenommen, um zu verstehen, dass Stress eine der Hauptursachen für Rückfälle ist, egal ob du 15 Tage oder 4.526 Tage nüchtern bist.

Werde niemals selbstgefällig.

Ich hätte es fast auf die harte Tour gelernt, nachdem ich einige Jahre lang nüchtern war und beschlossen hatte, mein erstes Buch zu veröffentlichen, umzuziehen und mir einen neuen Welpen zuzulegen – alles zur gleichen

Zeit! Ich hätte vielleicht nachgegeben, wenn ich nicht ein Buch über den Verzicht auf Alkohol veröffentlicht und die in diesem Buch erwähnten Werkzeuge benutzt hätte.

Es ist klar, dass du nicht jeden Trigger vermeiden kannst, außer du versteckst dich in einer Höhle. Und selbst wenn du das tätest, würde dein Verstand wahrscheinlich selbst einige Trigger finden! Aus diesem Grund findest du hier einige Strategien, um mit den Triggern umzugehen, die du nicht vermeiden kannst:

- **Suche dir die Unterstützung anderer.** Partner, Freunde, nüchterne Bekannte und Mitglieder von Online-Communitys können dir helfen, Situationen zu meistern, in denen du Versuchung widerstehen musst. Erstaunlich viele Menschen, die gerade nüchtern geworden sind, sitzen bei Hochzeiten an ihren Smartphones und holen sich online Unterstützung von anderen, während sie darum kämpfen, nicht nachzugeben.
- **Bleib bei deinem Gefühl.** Manchmal muss man es einfach „aussitzen". Vielleicht bist du es zum Beispiel gewohnt, deine sozialen Ängste zu

verdrängen, indem du zu Beginn eines Arbeitstreffens ein paar Drinks zu dir nimmst. Du wirst feststellen, dass dieses Gefühl *sowieso* vorbeigeht. Und es wird von Mal zu Mal leichter.

- **Erinnere dich an deine Gründe.** Mach es dir zur Gewohnheit, dich an deine Gründe für den Alkoholverzicht zu erinnern. Vielleicht hast du eine Notiz auf deinem Handy oder in deiner Tasche mit einer Liste der Gründe, warum du nüchtern bleiben willst. Du könntest dir sogar ein Tattoo stechen lassen!

- **Finde Ablenkungen.** Das Verlangen geht vorbei. Überlege dir eine Reihe von Aktivitäten, auf die du zurückgreifen kannst, wenn es dir schlecht geht. Unterschätze nicht die Macht eines zehnminütigen Spaziergangs um den Block oder eines kurzen Bummels durch eine Buchhandlung oder einen Plattenladen, um dir etwas von dem Geld zu gönnen, das du für Alkohol ausgegeben hättest.

- **Spiele die Zukunft im Kopf durch.** Das ist besonders nützlich, wenn du das (sehr verbreitete) Gefühl hast: „Es wird schon gut gehen, wenn ich nur ein oder zwei Drinks nehme". Überlege dir, was bei all den anderen Gelegenheiten passiert ist, bei denen du dir vorgenommen hast, nur „ein oder zwei" zu trinken. Dann überlege, wie du dich morgen früh fühlen wirst, wenn du deine Serie von nüchternen Tagen neu starten musst.

- **Geh einfach!** Wenn dir eine Situation zu viel wird, geh einfach. Es kann helfen (und deinen Stresspegel senken), wenn du im Voraus die Weichen stellst und den Leuten sagst, dass du früher gehen musst. Aber in Wirklichkeit ist das völlig egal. Die Leute, die noch getrunken haben, werden sich wahrscheinlich nicht daran erinnern – und selbst wenn sie es tun, werden sie zu verkatert sein, um sich darum zu kümmern!

Eine Übung zum Abschluss dieses Kapitels: Besorge dir einen Notizblock und lege ihn neben dein Bett. Dort kannst du Folgendes in drei Spalten auflisten: Menschen, Orte, Dinge.

Beginne mit einer Liste der Ereignisse, an die du dich erinnern kannst und die als Trigger wirken, und baue die Liste mit der Zeit aus. So kannst du deine Trigger **bewusst wahrnehmen** und kannst **positive Maßnahmen** ergreifen, um nüchtern zu bleiben und deine **Intuition** für zukünftige Ereignisse zu stärken.

Dies sind nur Beispiele (die vielleicht ein bisschen Wahrheit in sich tragen), die dir helfen sollen:

Menschen	Orte	Dinge
Tommy - Trinkkumpel	Die Taverne (Lokale Kneipe)	Gerüche, die mich an Urlaub erinnern (bestimmte Reinigungsmittel, seltsamerweise!)
Wendy - Trinkgefährtin bei der Arbeit	Das Haus meiner Nonna (da sie Italienerin ist, gab es immer Wein zu trinken und zu sehen)	Kleine Knopfbeutel, die man mit einem neuen Hemd/einer neuen Hose bekommt, erinnern mich an Drogenbeutel
Onkel Stan bei Familientreffen (Ja, Familie kann triggernd sein!)	In den Urlaub fahren (buchstäblich überall!)	Alkoholfreie Getränke (sie erinnern mich an alkoholische Versionen – aber das ist bei allen unterschiedlich)

Im nächsten Kapitel geht es um das große „Ich bin".

Es wird Zeit, dass wir über das Ego sprechen.

Kapitel 5:

Das nüchterne Ego – Verstehen und Zähmen des Egos

Das Ego ist das eigennützige „Ich", das sich von Kindheit an entwickelt. Unsere Erfahrungen mit der Welt fließen in unsere Gedanken ein. Aus diesen Gedanken entstehen wiederum Glaubenssätze, die bestimmen, wie wir mit der Welt umgehen.

Das Problem besteht darin, dass das Ego sich selbst übertreffen kann. Es kann sich schnell aufblähen, unsere Realität verzerren und uns dazu bringen, uns so zu verhalten, wie wir denken, dass wir sind, und nicht so, wie wir *tatsächlich* sind.

Aber ich kann dich beruhigen: Wie du gleich sehen wirst, ist es nicht unbedingt deine Schuld, wenn dein Ego dich dazu bringt, dich so zu verhalten, als wärst du das Zentrum des

Universums. Es ist nicht unbedingt deine Schuld, wenn fast jeder Satz, den du sagst, mit „Ich ..." beginnt.

Die Gesellschaft hat sich verschworen, um Menschen dazu zu bringen, so zu sein.

Dennoch ist es gefährlich, die Realität auf ein falsches Selbstverständnis zu gründen, wenn es nicht kontrolliert wird. Es ist nicht gut, blind zu sein für dein Ego und deine falschen Vorstellungen von deinem eigenen Wert für die Welt.

Lass uns herausfinden, warum das Problem auftritt und was wir dagegen tun können.

Der moderne Kapitalismus ist wie geschaffen dafür, dem Ego freien Lauf zu lassen. Jeder will mehr. Jeder will *besser* sein. Es wird aktiv gefördert und ist unausweichlich. Werbung und soziale Medien haben eine Menge zu verantworten.

Diese Rattenjagd existiert schon seit Jahrzehnten, doch heute findet sie zehnfach verstärkt statt.

In Kneipen, Bars und Clubs triffst du mit Sicherheit auf jede Menge Egos. Viele von ihnen ziehen (zu Recht oder zu Unrecht) Menschen an, die für ihre besonders übergroßen Egos bekannt sind: Banker, Immobilienmakler und Social-Media-Influencer. Egos folgen anderen Egos, und sie sind alle entschlossen, sich gegenseitig zu übertrumpfen!

Alkohol und Drogen sind Kryptonit für das Ego. Es ist auch ohne den Zusatz von Substanzen schon gefährlich genug. Wenn wir trinken, können wir auch „andere Egos" entwickeln. Bei manchen Menschen ändert sich der Charakter komplett, wenn sie ein paar Gläser getrunken haben. Das nennt sich „Jekyll und Hyde"-Effekt – der nüchterne Charakter einer Person ist völlig anders als das „Monster", zu dem die Person wird, wenn sie betrunken ist. Vielleicht kennst du das auch!

Es gibt „Wendy, die Trinkerin", die dafür bekannt ist, dass sie ihr Körpergewicht in Wein trinken kann. Sie glaubt, dass sie das „Leben und die Seele" ist – dafür ist sie einfach nur laut, frech und eine ständige Nervensäge.

Da drüben an der Bar steht „Tommy Tequila". Er schnupft eine Linie Salz, bevor er sich einen Tequila-Shot ins Auge schießt. Er hält sich für eine Legende, aber in Wirklichkeit ist er ein arroganter, selbstgerechter Idiot. Während er sich amüsiert, ruiniert er die Abende vieler Menschen in seiner Umgebung.

Es gibt bestimmte Verhaltensweisen, die auf ein übergroßes Ego hindeuten. Lästern über andere Menschen ist eines davon, und das hört man oft in der Kneipe. Andere Verhaltensweisen sind Arroganz, Schuldzuweisungen, Groll, nie im Unrecht zu sein, andere unterbrechen und die Lorbeeren für die Erfolge anderer einheimsen.

Das Ego kann dazu führen, dass wir uns selbst zu wichtig nehmen. Das führt dazu, dass wir uns über andere Menschen stellen und unbelehrbar werden.

Das ist das Rezept für Katastrophen.

Du liest dieses Buch, weil du Hilfe brauchst. Das ist auch gut so, denn du hast dein Ego beiseite geschoben, um zu lernen. Aber es ist immer noch da und wartet darauf, dich zu überwältigen.

Das Ego fühlt sich gerne wohl. Alles, was ihm Unbehagen bereitet, wird als Bedrohung empfunden. (Das ist vielleicht der Grund, warum „Tommy Tequila" dazu neigt, zu jedem, der seine betrunkenen Possen missbilligend

ansieht, „Was guckst du so?"
entgegenzuschmettern)

Der Schlüssel zum Erfolg im Leben und zur
Bewältigung von Herausforderungen liegt darin,
zu akzeptieren, dass du der Schüler bist, und
niemals der Meister bist. Im Leben auf der Erde
gibt es unendlich viel zu lernen, aber das Ego
denkt gerne, dass es nichts mehr zu verbessern
hat.

Wenn du das nächste Mal ein Feedback
bekommst, das dir nicht gefällt, stelle dir eine
einfache Frage: Gibt es *wirklich* nichts, was du
aus diesem Feedback lernen kannst, oder ist es
dein Ego, das sich verzweifelt verteidigen will?

Wenn ich an meine eigene Zeit als Trinker
zurückdenke, bin ich mir jetzt selbst bewusst,
dass mein ungesundes Selbstverständnis (mein
Ego) mir eine Menge Hindernisse in den Weg
gelegt hat. Es hinderte mich daran, mich in
andere einzufühlen, etwas über die Welt zu
lernen und Chancen zu erkennen. Ich traf viel zu
viele Entscheidungen auf der Grundlage der
Illusion, wer ich zu sein *glaubte*, und nicht, wer
ich *wirklich* war (oder tief im Inneren sein
wollte).

Das Ego spielt eine große Rolle dabei, warum Menschen rückfällig werden. Schließlich erreichen sie den Punkt, an dem sie denken, dass sie "okay" sind. Aber es ist das Ego, das spricht.

Hast du schon mal eine Diät gemacht, abgenommen und bist dann sofort wieder in dein altes Leben zurückgekehrt? Das ist das Ego, das sich selbst übertrifft (wozu es neigt). Es denkt, du hättest dein Ziel erreicht, obwohl du eigentlich noch viel weiter gehen müsstest.

Also besinnt sich dein Ego auf das, was am einfachsten ist. Iss, was du willst, wann du willst, und kümmere dich nicht darum, ins Fitnessstudio zu gehen. Dieses falsche Selbstbewusstsein hat sich wieder aufgeblasen und glaubt, es besser zu wissen. So kommst du wieder an den Punkt, an dem deine Hose zu eng ist, du dich fragst, wie du sie wieder anziehen sollst, und du rufst deinen Personal Trainer um Hilfe – SCHON WIEDER!

Denselben Prozess kannst du bei Menschen beobachten, die das Trinken aufgeben. Sie bekommen Komplimente, sie passen in die neuen Hosen, sie sehen jünger aus und sie haben mehr Geld, aber diejenigen, die ihr Ego nicht in den Griff bekommen, weil es sich zu sehr aufbläht und ein falsches Selbstwertgefühl entwickelt, fangen an zu glauben, dass es ihnen gut geht und sie trinken können. So schlimm wird es schon nicht sein.

Ein paar Wochen später geben sie dann nach. Der Kreislauf wiederholt sich: Kater > Bedauern > Wiederholung, bis sie sich wieder selbst stoppen (das könntest sogar du sein!).

Wenn du mit dem Trinken aufhörst, ohne dich um Selbsterkenntnis und Intuition zu bemühen, kannst du in einen Zustand des „trockenen Alkohols" geraten (ein Begriff, der in anonymen Gruppen oft diskutiert wird).

Stell dir noch einmal „Tommy Tequila" vor. Er könnte aufhören, Alkohol zu konsumieren, und trotzdem arrogant und selbstsüchtig bleiben und niemandem außer sich selbst gefallen wollen.

Es ist durchaus möglich, nüchtern zu sein und trotzdem ein Arschloch zu sein.

Wieder einmal ist die moderne Gesellschaft am Werk. Es ist ganz natürlich, dass das Ego versucht, wieder die Kontrolle zu übernehmen. Wir leben in einer Welt des Wettbewerbs und des „Schau mich an". Bis zu einem gewissen Grad brauchen wir unser Ego, wenn wir im

Leben vorankommen und gesehen und gehört werden wollen.

Dein Ego wird *immer* ein Teil von dir sein. Es kommt darauf an, wie du es beherrschst, zähmst und zu deinem Vorteil nutzt, damit du mit dem Trinken aufhören und nüchtern bleiben kannst.

So bekommst du dein Ego in den Griff und nutzt es zu deinem Vorteil

Wie kannst du nun dein Ego in den Griff bekommen? Hier sind einige effektive Möglichkeiten:

Beobachte dich und höre dir selbst zu

Arbeite daran, dir über die Dinge bewusst zu werden, die du sagst und die sich um „ich", „mein" und „mich" drehen. Was sagst du wirklich?

Wenn du dich dabei ertappst, dass du über jemanden lästerst, frage dich, was dich wirklich dazu veranlasst, diese Person herabzusetzen. Hast du vielleicht Angst, dass es ihnen besser gehen könnte als dir?

Das Ego hasst Angst, Unsicherheit und Eifersucht. Das Ego mag es nicht, wenn es sich unwohl fühlt. Aber oft reicht es schon aus, zu beobachten und zu merken, wenn das Ego ins Spiel kommt. Dadurch wird es gebändigt und gezähmt.

Noch einmal: Selbsterkenntnis ist der Schlüssel. Ohne Selbsterkenntnis erlaubst du deinem Ego, die vollständige Kontrolle zu übernehmen. Findest du Menschen liebenswert, denen es eindeutig nur um sich selbst geht? Das ist höchst unwahrscheinlich, aber wenn du von deinem Ego beherrscht wirst, wirst du zu diesen Menschen gehören.

Bleib bescheiden

Es gibt viele Möglichkeiten, bescheiden zu sein. Dazu gehört, anderen zu helfen, ohne eine Belohnung zu erwarten, Dankbarkeit zu üben, täglich ein Tagebuch zu führen und mehr zuzuhören als zu reden.

Feedback von anderen anzunehmen und zu verarbeiten (anstatt zu widersprechen) ist ebenfalls sehr wichtig, um sich selbst zu erden.

Erkenne deine Schwächen und gib zu, wenn du einen Fehler gemacht hast.

Sei offen zu lernen

Bedenke: Du bist der Schüler, nicht der Meister.

Alle, die dir auf der Straße begegnen, wissen einen Haufen Dinge, die du nicht weißt, und sind in bestimmten Dingen besser als du.

Eine besonders fiese Sache, die das Ego tut, ist zu verhindern, dass du die Hilfe bekommst, die du brauchst. Es kann dich aktiv daran hindern, ein Leben zu führen, auf das du stolz sein kannst.

Solltest du eine Therapie machen? Solltest du einen Entzug machen? Solltest du einem Familienmitglied gegenüber zugeben, dass du Hilfe brauchst? Dein Ego könnte dich davon abhalten, all diese Dinge zu tun, und hat es vielleicht sogar schon getan.

Bevor ich nüchtern wurde und als ich noch in der Unternehmenswelt arbeitete, war ich schrecklich darin, Feedback anzunehmen. Stattdessen habe ich gemeckert, gestöhnt und Ausreden gefunden.

Dann kam der Tag der Prämie, und ich bekam nie eine Prämie, die den Erwartungen meines Egos entsprach. Meine Standardreaktion war, dass ich mich nach anderen Jobs umsah. Sicherlich würde mir jemand anders das zahlen, was ich meiner Meinung nach wert war!

Erst jetzt weiß ich, dass ein Großteil des Feedbacks fair und richtig war. Hätte ich tatsächlich zugehört und die Ratschläge angenommen, wäre ich schon viel früher ein besserer Mensch geworden.

Es gibt niemanden, von dem du nicht etwas lernen kannst.

Vermeide Ego-Kämpfe

Konkurrenzdenken und „mit den anderen mithalten" ist eine Krankheit des modernen Kapitalismus.

Es gibt kaum etwas Langweiligeres als wetteifernde Gespräche über den Wert von Häusern, Gehältern und den Kauf neuer Autos, doch das ist alles Teil unserer „Höher, schneller, weiter"-Kultur. Leider wird das Ego in der Regel in diese Gespräche hineingezogen, selbst wenn du sie nicht selbst anstößt.

Der beste Weg, diese Situationen zu entschärfen, ist, so wenig wie möglich zu reagieren, wenn sie auftauchen. Versuche niemals, sie selbst zu initiieren. Wenn ein Gespräch das Ego der anderen Person nicht beflügelt, wird es bald im Sande verlaufen.

Nicht nur reden, sondern tun!

Um Menschen zu beeindrucken, musst du nicht über deine Erfolge reden, sondern sie erreichen.

Noch besser ist es, die Dinge zu erreichen, die dir wichtig sind, und sich nicht darum zu kümmern, ob jemand beeindruckt sein wird oder nicht. Du hast immer die Wahl: „Sein oder Tun". Die richtige Wahl gibt dir den Fokus und hält dich auf dem Boden.

Jage nicht den Likes hinterher

Social-Media-Plattformen sind so konzipiert, dass sie süchtig machen und dir das Gefühl geben, geliebt zu werden. Sie sollen emotionale Reaktionen hervorrufen, und Likes halten die Leute dazu an, wiederzukommen.

Vor allem Nüchternheits-Communitys können unglaublich unterstützend sein. Aber übertreibe es nicht mit der Jagd nach Likes, Liebe und Streicheleinheiten. Das kann süchtig machen und dein Selbstwertgefühl aufblähen.

Das Ego kommt in den sozialen Medien voll auf seine Kosten. Sei also vorsichtig, wie viel du davon zulässt.

Präsentiere die Fakten

Egos geben nicht gerne nach, wenn sie meinen „Recht" zu haben – selbst wenn sie eindeutig im Unrecht sind. Das ist verrückt.

Lass dich nicht in sinnlose Streitigkeiten verwickeln – weder mit deinem eigenen Ego noch mit dem von anderen. Wir alle haben Google in der Tasche – wir können es benutzen, die richtigen Antworten finden und weitermachen.

Nutze dein Alter Ego POSITIV

Nicht alle Alter Egos sind so lästig wie „Tommy Tequila" und „Wendy, die Trinkerin". Aber wir alle brauchen etwas Ego, um uns in der Welt, in der wir leben, zurechtzufinden. Ein gesundes Alter Ego, das uns hilft, stressige und herausfordernde Situationen zu meistern, kann uns gute Dienste leisten – solange es sorgfältig gemanagt wird!

In seinem Buch "Ich hinter der Maske" beschreibt Tyson Fury, der beste

Schwergewichtsboxer der Welt, wie sein Alter Ego – „The Gypsy King" – ihm zu solchen Höhenflügen verholfen hat. Jedes Mal, wenn er die Handschuhe anzog, kam diese andere Person zum Vorschein. Er war selbstbewusst, furchtlos und voller Angeberei – genau das, was man braucht, um auf diesem Niveau zu gewinnen.

Aber Tyson Fury ist ein Ehemann und Familienvater – nicht jemand, der von Ruhm und Reichtum besessen ist.

Solange du nicht zu deinem Alter Ego wirst, kann es ein mächtiges Werkzeug in beruflichen und gesellschaftlichen Situationen sein, wenn du ein bisschen mehr aus dir herauskommen musst. Vergiss aber nicht, ein Auge auf dein Ego zu haben, um sicherzustellen, dass du nicht in alte Muster zurückfällst.

Sei nicht wie Tommy Tequila oder Wendy, die Trinkerin.

Zu verstehen, wie dein Ego funktioniert, ist wichtig, um deine **Selbstwahrnehmung** zu stärken. So bleibst du lernfähig und kannst verhindern, dass du dich über andere stellst. Wenn du dich für **positive Maßnahmen** entscheidest, um mit deinem Ego umzugehen, bleibst du geerdet und deine **Intuition** ist auf dem richtigen Weg.

Im Laufe deines Lebens wird dein Ego immer wieder auftauchen. Es braucht Arbeit und Ausdauer, um es zu entkräften.

Hier ist eine kurze Übung zum Abschluss dieses Kapitels:

Wenn du dich das nächste Mal dabei ertappst, wie du über jemanden meckerst und jammerst, solltest du dir überlegen, wie du über ihn oder sie sprichst und wie der Kontext der Situation ist.

Frag dich in dieser Situation: Was ist es, das mich an mir selbst so unzufrieden macht?

Denn das wird immer der wahre Grund sein, warum du über andere Menschen meckerst und jammerst.

Im nächsten Kapitel sprechen wir über Taktiken. Ein nüchternes Leben bedeutet, mit den schlechten Tagen, den guten Tagen, den herausfordernden Tagen und den leichteren Tagen umzugehen. Es bedeutet auch, das alles ohne eine ungesunde „Stütze" zu tun, die dir dabei „hilft".

Es ist an der Zeit, dich wirklich auf die Dinge zu konzentrieren, die dir helfen, nüchtern zu *bleiben*.

KAPITEL 6:

ALTE GEWOHNHEITEN ÖFFNEN KEINE NEUEN TÜREN. METHODEN, DIE HELFEN, RÜCKFÄLLE ZU VERHINDERN UND DEINE NÜCHTERNHEIT ZU STÄRKEN

Du kannst immer damit rechnen, dass das Leben eine Menge Höhen und Tiefen bereithält. Wie bereits erwähnt, ist die Nüchternheit an manchen Tagen einfach und an anderen sehr viel herausfordernder. Das gilt sowohl für die dauerhafte Nüchternheit als auch für die Anfangszeit.

Nicht zu trinken wird mit der Zeit immer natürlicher. Du kannst Wochen oder Monate durchhalten, ohne überhaupt daran zu denken. Aber unerwartete Belastungen und noch nicht bewältigte Trigger können von überall her kommen. Das kann alles Mögliche sein – von einem Trauerfall bis hin zu deinem ersten nüchternen Ausflug in ein All-Inclusive-Resort.

Sehen wir uns einige der Möglichkeiten an, wie du deine Nüchternheit wirklich stärken und einen zukünftigen Rückfall verhindern kannst.

Die Einstellung der Dankbarkeit

Dankbarkeit funktioniert. Ich werde gleich erklären, warum.

Der kapitalistische Lebensstil und die Rattenjagd sorgen dafür, dass wir immer mehr wollen. Das ist Teil unserer Konditionierung. Wir kaufen ein Haus und bemerken sofort, wenn die Nachbarn Anbauten, Wintergärten realisieren oder neuere Autos vor dem Haus parken.

Egal wie lange wir für das Haus gespart haben, es ist plötzlich nicht mehr gut genug.

Es überrascht nicht, dass unser Ego dabei voll mitmacht, und der Kreislauf des „mehr mehr mehr" setzt sich fort.

Es ist kein Wunder, dass so viele Menschen zum Alkohol greifen, weil er betäubend wirkt. Doch das führt zu einem toxischen Chaos. Du bist unglücklich darüber, dass du nicht all das „Mehr" hast, das du dir wünschst, und du konsumierst eine Substanz, die dich deines Potenzials beraubt. Am Ende bist du unglücklich und fängst an, dich über alles und jeden zu ärgern.

Sobald ich in die Arbeitswelt eintrat, stürzte ich mich direkt in mein eigenes Rennen. Ich war ständig von der Zukunft geblendet und nie zufrieden mit dem, was ich zu diesem Zeitpunkt hatte. Es kam mir nicht einmal in den Sinn, meinen Eltern für alles zu danken, was sie getan hatten, um mich an diesen Punkt zu bringen.

Ich hatte ein Dach über dem Kopf, einen sicheren Job sowie eine gesunde Familie und Freunde. Trotzdem war ich nie dankbar für all das. Stattdessen schaute ich auf andere und beneidete sie um das, was sie hatten. Ich hatte nie das Gefühl, dass ich genügend der „glänzenden Dinge" hatte.

Ich wusste nicht, dass Dankbarkeit ein einfacher Schlüssel dazu ist, viel glücklicher zu sein – und ich dann auch weniger geneigt bin, meine Sorgen zu ertränken, weil ich nicht die Dinge hatte, die ich haben „musste".

Dankbarkeit funktioniert viel besser als Schnaps. Sie ist ein völlig kostenloses Werkzeug, das Neid, Unzufriedenheit und Anspruchsdenken abwehrt. Diese starken Emotionen können in jeder Phase der Nüchternheit zu einem Rückfall führen, nicht nur am Anfang.

Die Forschung zeigt, dass das Praktizieren von Dankbarkeit „zu mehr Gesundheit, Glück und Weisheit in uns selbst und in unserer Gemeinschaft beitragen kann".[32] Eine Studie mit einer Gruppe von Menschen, die eine einfache tägliche Dankbarkeitsübung durchführten, zeigte zum Beispiel, dass sie „deutlich glücklicher und weniger deprimiert" waren. Dieser Effekt hielt auch noch Monate nach Abschluss der Übung an.

Dankbarkeit ist ein wichtiger Bestandteil der Zwölf-Schritte-Programme. Diese Programme haben dazu beigetragen, einige der schlimmsten Säufer und Süchtigen der Gesellschaft in mitfühlende, nüchterne Helden zu verwandeln, die ihr Leben komplett umgekrempelt haben. Das ist zu mächtig, um es zu ignorieren.

Ich praktiziere Dankbarkeit, seit ich nüchtern bin. Sie hält mich auf dem Boden, macht mich demütig und gibt mir eine neue Perspektive. Ich kann aber nicht behaupten, dass sich materielle Dinge nicht in mein Leben geschlichen haben.

Ich praktiziere Dankbarkeit, seit ich nüchtern bin. Sie hält mich auf dem Boden der Tatsachen, macht mich demütig und schenkt mir eine neue Perspektive. Ich kann nicht behaupten, dass sich materielle Dinge nicht wieder in mein Leben geschlichen haben. Aber es ist die Dankbarkeit, die verhindert, dass der „betrunkene Schwachkopf Sean" (und sein großes Ego) wieder auftaucht.

Wenn du dankbar für die Dinge bist, die du hast, werden alle anderen „Wünsche" weniger wichtig. Das hat zur Folge, dass sie dich emotional nicht mehr so stark beeinflussen können. Das ist eine große Sache, denn so ist es viel unwahrscheinlicher, dass du den großen roten „Sch**ß drauf"-Knopf drückst und rückfällig wirst.

Wie kannst du Dankbarkeit praktizieren?

Dazu gehören zwei einfache Schritte[33]:

1. Nimm dir Zeit, die Dinge zu würdigen, für die du dankbar bist.
2. Lerne, dass die meisten Dinge, für die du dankbar bist, nicht aus dir selbst

kommen, sondern von anderen Menschen oder Dingen – deiner Familie, deinen Haustieren, der Welt oder dem Universum.

Eine gute Möglichkeit, damit anzufangen, ist, dir anzugewöhnen, jeden Tag drei Dinge aufzuschreiben, für die du dankbar bist. Du kannst das auf jede Art und Weise tun, die für dich funktioniert. Beliebte Methoden sind sie z.B. morgens beim Zähneputzen im Kopf zu notieren oder jeden Abend einen Notizblock (oder ein Dankbarkeitstagebuch) zu benutzen.

Hier sind ein paar Dinge, die du auf eine tägliche Liste schreiben könntest:

- Ich bin dankbar, dass ich nüchtern aufgewacht bin.
- Ich bin dankbar dafür, dass ich ohne Kater / Kopfschmerzen / das dringende Bedürfnis, auf die Toilette zu rennen(!), aufgewacht bin.
- Ich bin dankbar, dass die Sonne scheint.
- Ich bin dankbar für die Liebe und Unterstützung durch meine Familie.
- Ich bin dankbar, dass meine Kinder glücklich und gesund sind.

- Ich bin dankbar, dass ich Hobbys habe, auf die ich mich freuen kann.

In der obigen Liste findest du keine Aussagen wie „Ich bin dankbar für meinen BMW" oder „Ich bin dankbar für meine große, glänzende Rolex". Das liegt daran, dass oberflächliche und materialistische Dankbarkeit nicht viel Kraft hat.

Beachte, dass die Beispiele den zweiten Schritt berücksichtigen – dankbar zu sein für Dinge, die von außen kommen.

Es ist wichtig, tiefe, bedeutungsvolle Dankbarkeit zu üben. „Ich bin dankbar für meine Katze" ist eine relativ bedeutungslose Aussage. Denk darüber nach, warum du für deine Katze dankbar bist – die Tatsache, dass sie dich tröstet und sicher fühlen lässt – oder vielleicht sogar die Tatsache, dass du dir keine Sorgen über Ungeziefer in deinem Haus machen musst!

Tiefe Dankbarkeit bringt tiefgreifende, starke Emotionen hervor.

Wie auch immer du dich entscheidest, Dankbarkeit zu praktizieren, Beständigkeit ist entscheidend. Das ist ein weiterer dieser positiven Kreisläufe, die Wiederholungen belohnen. Und es funktioniert – die Wissenschaft und die Erfahrung von Millionen von Menschen auf der ganzen Welt, die es praktizieren, zeigen das.

Lass „JOMO" in dein Leben

Wir alle haben schon von „FOMO" (Fear of Missing Out) gehört. JOMO (Joy of Missing Out) ist das aufgeklärte Pendent zu FOMO, nur viel besser.

Angst ist ein starkes Gefühl, das uns dazu verleiten kann, die große Nacht erleben zu wollen. Aber was wirst du wirklich verpassen? Dass du vergisst, worüber du geredet hast, und dir dann Sorgen machst, worüber du geredet hast? Den Kater? Die übermäßigen Ausgaben? Die Ziele, an denen du nicht gearbeitet hast, weil du keine Motivation mehr hattest?

Zum Vergleich die „JOMO"-Alternative: Du wachst auf und weißt genau, was du am Abend zuvor gemacht hast. Du bist früh aufgestanden, hast keinen Kater und bist bereit, etwas zu schaffen. Du hast mehr Geld auf der Bank und nicht weniger. Du bist motiviert, das zu tun, was du wirklich tun willst – egal ob du an einem lebensverändernden Projekt arbeitest oder einem Hobby frönst.

Sowohl FOMO als auch JOMO spielen in den Kreisläufen eine Rolle. Ich überlasse es dir, herauszufinden, was positiv und was negativ ist! Mit der Zeit kann eine wiederholte Entscheidung, Grenzen zu setzen, „Nein" zu sagen und der Fahrer statt der Beifahrer zu sein, die Richtung deines Lebens drastisch verändern.

Das heißt nicht, dass du nie mehr ausgehst! Der Unterschied besteht darin, dass du anfängst, auszugehen, wenn du es willst, und nicht, wenn du fälschlicherweise denkst, dass du es *musst*.

Verbinden wir all das mit dem, was du bisher gelernt hast:

- Eine gute **Selbstwahrnehmung** bedeutet, dass du weißt, dass du die Verhaltensmuster, die dich dazu gebracht haben, dieses Buch zu lesen, wahrscheinlich wiederholen wirst, wenn du ohne einen Plan zum Nüchternbleiben ausgehst.
- **Positiv zu handeln** (oder in diesem Fall nicht zu handeln) bedeutet, „Nein" zu sagen, dem Gruppenzwang zu widerstehen und das zu tun, was für DICH richtig ist.
- **Intuition** zu entwickeln bedeutet, aus den Zeiten zu lernen, in denen du die

richtigen Entscheidungen triffst: „Ich habe mich letztes Wochenende gut gefühlt; ich will mich wieder gut fühlen."

Limitierende Glaubenssätze vs. positive Affirmationen

Wir haben uns bereits damit beschäftigt, wie wichtig es ist, sich selbst wichtige Fragen zu stellen.

Hier ist eine für dich:

Wenn du nicht stark vom Alkohol abhängig bist und eine medizinisch überwachte Entgiftung brauchst - **was ist deine Ausrede dafür, dass du bisher nicht nüchtern geworden bist?**

Die meisten regelmäßigen Trinker werden eine schnelle Antwort haben: „Ich habe eine Scheidung durchgemacht." „Die Arbeit war herausfordernd." „Einem Familienmitglied ging es nicht gut." „Ich war sehr gestresst!"

All das sind limitierende Glaubenssätze und – ehrlich gesagt – sind sie Unsinn. Alkohol hat eine Scheidung noch nie einfacher gemacht. Alkohol hat es noch nie einfacher gemacht, bei der Arbeit erfolgreich zu sein. Alkohol macht es nicht einfacher, sich um kranke Verwandte zu kümmern. Und wie gut dokumentiert und wissenschaftlich bewiesen ist, macht Alkohol Menschen viel gestresster und depressiver.

Solange du am Leben bist, hoffst du, deine Lebenssituation umzukehren, egal ob es sich um Alkohol, Drogen, einen Bankrott, eine schlimme Trennung, den Tod eines Familienmitglieds oder eine andere Herausforderung handelt, der du gegenüberstehst.

Sei dankbar, dass du noch Hoffnung hast. Denn wenn du tot bist, hast du keine Hoffnung mehr.

Auch wenn du im Gefängnis sitzt, hast du Hoffnung. Wenn du in der Reha bist, hast du Hoffnung. Wenn du dieses Buch liest, nachdem du jahrelang rückfällig geworden bist, hast du Hoffnung.

Hoffnung ist der Katalysator für Veränderungen.

Limitierende Glaubenssätze halten uns davon ab, sinnvolle Veränderungen vorzunehmen. Sie nähren unseren inneren Monolog – die Gedanken, die zu unseren Überzeugungen werden. Aber Gedanken sind zunächst nichts anderes.

Du hast Hoffnung und du hast eine Wahl.

Du kannst dir sagen: „Ich bin eine wertlose alkoholkranke Person", und du wirst eine und bleibst eine.

Oder du kannst dir sagen: „Ich bin in der Lage, mich vom Alkohol zu befreien und werde mein bestes Leben leben", und tust genau das.

Mag sein, dass dir das zu simpel erscheint. Natürlich ist es nicht ganz so einfach, anders zu denken und sich über Nacht zu verändern. Aber eigentlich ist es auch nicht viel komplizierter. Alles, was du verstehen musst, ist, dass einschränkende Glaubenssätze als großer Faktor bewirken, dass du in einem negativen Kreislauf um den Alkohol stecken bleibst.

„Ich bin nicht gut genug. Also werde ich mich betrinken."

„Ich kann diese Arbeit nicht machen. Also werde ich mich betrinken."

„Ich werde meinem Bruder oder meiner Schwester nie gerecht werden. Also werde ich mich betrinken."

All das sind einschränkende Glaubenssätze. Du solltest sie erkennen, dir ihrer bewusst werden und sie ändern. Eine gute Möglichkeit, das zu tun, ist, sie durch positive Affirmationen zu ersetzen.

Das erste, was mir in der Reha beigebracht wurde, war, mich vor einen Spiegel zu stellen, mir in die Augen zu sehen und eine Reihe von positiven Affirmationen zu wiederholen.

Wenn dich der Gedanke daran erschaudern lässt, kannst du dir sicher sein, dass es mir ähnlich ging. Vor einem Spiegel zu stehen und Dinge zu sagen wie „Ich bin selbstbewusst und fähig" wirkt besonders lächerlich, wenn du kein Wort von dem glaubst, was du sagst.

Aber die Sache ist die, dass Menschen im Entzug fast immer an ihrem Tiefpunkt ankommen. Mein innerer Monolog war zu diesem Zeitpunkt gefährlich negativ. Ich sagte mir ständig, dass ich nicht gut genug sei – und das hielt mich in einem negativen Feedback-Kreislauf. Wenn du dir selbst sagst, dass du unwürdig, nicht liebenswert und unfähig bist, wird das zu einer sich selbst erfüllenden Prophezeiung.

Hier sind einige Beispiele für einschränkende Glaubenssätze und die positiven Affirmationen, die du verwenden kannst, um ihnen entgegenzuwirken.

Limitierender Glaubenssatz	Positive Affirmation
Ich bin ein negativer Mensch.	Ich bin ein positiver Mensch.
Ich werde nicht geliebt.	Ich bin fähig, geliebt zu werden.
Ohne Alkohol bin ich langweilig.	Ich bin mehr als genug, wenn ich nüchtern bin.
Ich bin nicht selbstbewusst.	Ich bin selbstbewusst und fähig.
Ich werde nie erfolgreich sein.	Ich kann alles erreichen, worauf ich hinarbeite.

Wenn du darüber nachdenkst, würdest du nie mit einem Freund oder einer geliebten Person so reden, wie du mit dir selbst redest. Aber unglückliche Trinkende bleiben oft jahrelang in ihren einschränkenden Überzeugungen gefangen. Diese Überzeugungen können schon in der Kindheit verankert worden sein (und es lohnt sich, *dem* auf den Grund zu gehen).

Also trau dich, vor den Spiegel zu treten und den Prozess der Neuverdrahtung deines Gehirns in Gang zu setzen. Die Qualität deines Lebens hängt von der Qualität deiner Gedanken ab, also arbeite hart daran, der Negativität den Garaus zu machen. Wiederhole es täglich, um maximale Ergebnisse zu erzielen.

Ich kann nicht leugnen, dass ich zusammenzuckte, als ich zum ersten Mal mit positiven Affirmationen konfrontiert wurde, aber sie funktionieren. Wenn sie nicht funktionieren würden, würde ich immer noch trinken und mir sagen, wie nutzlos ich bin.

Deine **Selbstwahrnehmung** wird sich deiner eigenen einschränkenden Überzeugungen bewusst – denk daran: Wenn du eine Ausrede dafür findest, etwas nicht zu tun, ist das deine einschränkende Überzeugung. Frage dich selbst, wenn du dich mit deinen einschränkenden Glaubenssätzen auseinandersetzt: Stimmt das?

Wenn du dir dieser Ausreden bewusst wirst, kannst du **positive Maßnahmen** ergreifen, die dir helfen, dein Ziel, nicht zu trinken und nüchtern zu bleiben, zu erreichen.

Diese Fähigkeiten werden sich in der Praxis bewähren, und du wirst auf deine **Intuition** bauen, um dich bei zukünftigen Ausreden zu ertappen und dich fast schon unbewusst zu fragen: „Stimmt das?" Dann kannst du endlich die Ausreden hinter dir lassen und automatisch etwas tun.

Der Blick in die Kristallkugel des Trinkens

Alkohol trinken ist eines der wenigen Dinge im Leben (neben Steuern zahlen und dem Tod), von denen wir mit großer Sicherheit wissen, dass sie SEHR wiederholbare Folgen haben. Du brauchst keine Kristallkugel, um zu wissen, was passieren wird, aber ein Blick in die Zukunft hilft dir, denselben Albtraum nicht mehr auf Autopilot zu erleben.

Etwas, das du in Nüchternheitsforen häufig hörst, ist „der Blick in die Zukunft" Er bezieht sich auf die Fähigkeit der Visualisierung.

Die Visualisierung ist mit der Selbstwahrnehmung verbunden. Es geht darum zu lernen, bewusst vorauszudenken, um Trigger und schwierige Situationen zu umgehen.

Wenn du an deinen Visualisierungsfähigkeiten arbeitest, kannst du dir eine Menge Ärger ersparen.

Angenommen, du bist in der dritten Woche deiner Nüchternheit und deine Freunde versuchen, dich zu „ein paar Drinks" zu verleiten.

Schau in die Zukunft.

Waren es jemals nur ein paar? Nein, natürlich nicht. Du hast wahrscheinlich jahrelang solide Beweise dafür gesammelt, dass es sich eher um eine durchzechte Nacht handelt.

Was passiert danach? Ein Streit? Eine Schlägerei? Ein Kater? Du vergisst, was du gesagt hast, weißt aber, dass es peinlich war? Ein geleertes Bankkonto? Ein oder zwei Tage

krankgeschrieben von der Arbeit?
Möglicherweise all das oben Genannte?

Wenn du dir diese möglichen Szenarien vor
Augen führst, kannst du die richtigen
Maßnahmen ergreifen. Das kann bedeuten, dass
du die Einladung ablehnst (und dir JOMO
gönnst).

Zu den Strategien kann auch ein „Exit-Plan"
gehören, der sicherstellt, dass du nüchtern aus
der Situation herauskommst. Lege zum Beispiel
fest, wo du nach zwei Stunden sein musst und
dass du dorthin fahren musst. Oder beschließe
im Voraus, dass du gehen wirst, sobald deine
Freunde ihren dritten Drink zu sich genommen
haben – du wirst wahrscheinlich merken, dass
du dann sowieso gehen möchtest!

Es kann hilfreich sein, sich auf die Emotionen zu
konzentrieren, wenn du „in die Zukunft blickst".
Indem du dir die Situation im Voraus ausmalst
und darüber nachdenkst, wie du dich fühlen
wirst, trainierst du dein Gehirn, *bevor* du in die
Situation gerätst. Ermutige dich also, dir
vorzustellen, wie peinlich es ist, die betrunkenste
Person auf der Hochzeit zu sein, oder wie es ist,
am Montagmorgen wackelig zur Arbeit zu
stolpern. Das ist unheimlich effektiv.

Das Tolle an der Visualisierung ist, dass sie in beide Richtungen funktioniert. Du kannst also nicht nur das Band mit den Dingen, die du nicht tun willst (und die nicht passieren sollen), vorspulen, sondern dir auch die positiven Folgen besserer Entscheidungen vorstellen.

Nehmen wir die Hochzeit als Beispiel: Du könntest dir vorstellen, wie du am Morgen danach aufwachst und dich an jeden Moment erinnerst – auch an die vielen Male, an denen dir gesagt wurde, wie gut du aussiehst! Du könntest dir die Person vorstellen, die am meisten getrunken hat, und wie sie sich danach fühlen wird. Und vielleicht – nur dieses eine Mal – könntest du dein Ego verwöhnen und dir vorstellen, wie die Leute von deiner neuen Nüchternheit beeindruckt sind.

Während du dir das vorstellst, stellst du einige wichtige neuronale Verbindungen her. Du hilfst deinem Gehirn dabei, Freude mit NICHT-Trinken zu verbinden. Du fängst an, die jahrelangen Denkfehler zu reparieren.

Und – was vielleicht am wichtigsten ist – du machst es viel wahrscheinlicher, dass du die Hochzeit stolz, nüchtern und nicht peinlich betrunken überstehst.

In seinem Buch „How Champions Think" beschreibt der Sportpsychologe Dr. Bob Rotella eine Eigenschaft, die einige der erfolgreichsten Sportstars der Welt gemeinsam haben. Sie stellen sich oft vor, wie sie einen Wettkampf gewinnen, bevor sie das Tafelsilber in den Händen halten. Die Nerven haben sie bereits durchlebt, viele Male in ihrem eigenen Kopf. Das eigentliche Ereignis fällt ihnen dann viel leichter und sie können die Trophäe endlich in der Realität in Empfang nehmen.

Wenn du dir vorstellst, dass du eine betrunkene Veranstaltung ohne Kater überstehst, kannst du dir deine „Nüchtern-Trophäe" für 24 alkoholfreie Stunden abholen.

Wenn du aufgrund deiner **Selbstwahrnehmung** über potenzielle Gefahren auf dem Weg Bescheid weißt, kannst du dir ein Bild machen und vorausplanen.

Wenn du die potenziellen Gefahren kennst, kannst du sie umgehen und die entsprechenden **positiven Maßnahmen** ergreifen, ohne dein Hauptziel aus den Augen zu verlieren, nämlich nüchtern zu bleiben.

Wenn du auf ein paar Veranstaltungen warst und diese Werkzeuge benutzt hast, wirst du eine ernüchternde **Intuition** dafür entwickeln, wie frühere Veranstaltungen abgelaufen sind. Du wirst ein Gespür dafür bekommen, was gut funktioniert hat, was nicht und wann es der richtige Zeitpunkt ist, zu gehen, um deine Nüchternheit zu schützen.

Hör auf, Menschen „mietfrei in deinem Kopf wohnen zu lassen"

Du MUSST aufhören, dir Gedanken darüber zu machen, was die Leute denken.

Das raubt dir Energie und macht dich ängstlich – zwei Dinge, die dich zurück in den negativen Kreislauf des Trinkens treiben können.

Niemand interessiert sich wirklich dafür, ob du Alkohol trinkst oder nicht, aber viele Menschen, die nüchtern werden, machen sich Gedanken darüber, wie sie es erklären sollen. Die Realität ist, dass die Leute es oft nicht bemerken oder nicht danach fragen – und wenn sie doch fragen, hören sie bald auf zu fragen.

Wenn es dich stört, kannst du immer eine Antwort auf die Frage „Warum trinkst du nicht?" vorbereiten. „Ich mag die Person, die ich bin, wenn ich nüchtern bin" ist normalerweise mehr als genug, um die Leute davon abzuhalten, nachzuforschen.

Sich darüber zu sorgen, was die Leute denken, geht weit über die Sorge hinaus, wie sie deine Entscheidung, nicht zu trinken, beurteilen könnten. Sich davon zu befreien, was andere Leute denken, ist der Schlüssel, um sich als Person weiterzuentwickeln.

Es ist weit verbreitet, dass Menschen ihr Glück davon abhängig machen, was andere über sie denken.

Das ist ein lächerliches Konzept.

Wir überschätzen bei weitem, wie viel Zeit jemand damit verbringt, über uns zu denken!

Hier sind zwei Dinge, die du erkennen kannst:

1. Die Leute haben ihren eigenen Sch**ß zu erledigen und kämpfen ihre eigenen Kämpfe im Leben. Sie haben einfach nicht so viel Zeit, um über dich nachzudenken.
2. Glücklichsein ist eine innere Angelegenheit. Du kannst anderen Menschen nicht die Macht geben, zu

bestimmen, ob du glücklich bist oder nicht.

Dies zu lernen, kann dir helfen, mit dem Trinken aufzuhören. Sich langfristig an diese Glaubenssätze zu erinnern, kann dein Leben verändern.

Fortschritt statt Perfektion

Hast du versagt, wenn du 99 Tage lang nüchtern bleibst und dich an Tag 100 betrinkst?

Es mag sich so anfühlen, aber du hast absolut nicht versagt. Tatsächlich hast du es geschafft, in diesem Zeitraum 99 % der Zeit nüchtern zu bleiben.

Die erfolgreichsten Menschen auf der Welt sind diejenigen, die einfach durchhalten, egal, was auf sie zukommt. Sie stehen wieder auf, wenn sie niedergeschlagen wurden.

Aus einem Rückfall kannst du eine Menge lernen. Es ist also ein guter Zeitpunkt, um ein paar wichtige Fragen zu stellen:

- Was hat mich dazu bewogen, zu trinken?

- Was hat mich dazu veranlasst, die Flasche Wein zu öffnen? (Hol deinen Notizblock raus!)
- Was hat mich dazu veranlasst, zu trinken?

Bewerte dich selbst, bewerbe dich neu und mach weiter. Sei nachsichtig mit dir selbst. Es ist schon schwer genug, in einer alkoholisierten Welt nüchtern zu werden, in der alle vom Alkohol besessen zu sein scheinen. Also mach dich nicht fertig, wenn du fällst – steh wieder auf und mach weiter.

Wichtig ist, dass du dein vermeintliches „Versagen" nicht als Ausrede benutzt, um sofort wieder in dein altes Verhalten zurückzufallen und in Selbstmitleid zu schwelgen.

Wenn du einen Rückfall erleidest, hast du die Wahl: Du kannst im Rückfallmodus bleiben und weiter auf den „Sch**ß drauf"-Knopf drücken, oder du kannst dich entscheiden, deine Nüchternheit am nächsten Tag wieder aufzunehmen. Du hast die Macht zu entscheiden, was du tust. Der eine Weg ist positiv, der andere negativ!

Deine **Selbstwahrnehmung** zeigt, dass ein Rückfall nicht das Ende der Welt ist. Nichts an der Nüchternheit (oder am Leben) ist perfekt.

Stattdessen ist es eine großartige Möglichkeit, etwas zu lernen und eine Situation, die wir alle (unzählige Male!) durchgemacht haben.

Wenn du verstehst, dass es sich um Fortschritt und nicht um Perfektion handelt, kannst du dich von Rückfällen erholen und **positive Maßnahmen** ergreifen, um wieder auf die Beine zu kommen (im Sinne der Nüchternheit!).

Je mehr du weißt und tust, desto mehr wird deine **Intuition** wachsen, und jeder Rückfall wird dir ein paar Informationen liefern, die dir helfen, zukünftige Rückfälle zu überwinden.

Prokrastination vermeiden

Wie oft hast du schon gesagt: „Nach Weihnachten höre ich auf" oder „Nach den Feiertagen gebe ich mir einen Gesundheitskick"?

Es passiert einfach nicht, oder?

Wenn du ein besseres Leben willst, warum schiebst du es auf?

Es wird immer einen Geburtstag geben, eine Hochzeit, eine Grillparty, Freunde, die zu Besuch kommen, oder irgendein unerwartetes Ereignis, das du feiern oder bedauern möchtest.

Fang einfach an – einen Tag nach dem anderen.

Wenn du scheiterst, „scheitere vorwärts". Dann stehst du wieder auf und fängst von vorne an. Du baust immer noch dein Selbstbewusstsein auf und lernst, wie viel besser es sich anfühlt, voller Energie aufzuwachen, anstatt voller Bedauern.

Willst du wirklich ein besseres Leben, aber „noch nicht jetzt"? Wenn du ehrlich zu dir selbst bist, macht das keinen Sinn.

Alkoholfreie Verbindlichkeit

Rechenschaftspflicht ist unglaublich wichtig, wenn du mit dem Alkohol aufhörst. Sie ist der Eckpfeiler des Modells einer Patenschaft der Anonymen Alkoholiker – und sie funktioniert.

Wenn du dich entschlossen hast, einen ganzen Monat lang Sport zu treiben und dich fit zu halten, könntest du versuchen, es allein mit deiner Willenskraft zu schaffen. Oder du könntest einen Trainer engagieren und ein "Köperveränderungspaket" abschließen (und dafür bezahlen).

Bei der zweiten Option ist es viel wahrscheinlicher, dass du es durchziehst. Du hast Verantwortung übernommen. Du wirst den Trainer (oder die anderen Gruppenmitglieder) nicht im Stich lassen wollen. Du wirst das Geld, das du ausgegeben hast, nicht verschwenden wollen. Und du hast einen Profi, der dich auf Kurs hält und dich ermutigt.

Genauso ist es, wenn du mit dem Trinken aufhörst. Es ist nicht unmöglich, allein nüchtern zu werden, aber in der Realität ist es schwieriger.

Es lohnt sich, nach Unterstützung und Verantwortung zu suchen. Die harte Wahrheit ist, dass du diese wahrscheinlich nicht von deiner Familie, deinen Freunden oder Kollegen bekommst – vor allem, wenn es die Leute sind, mit denen du normalerweise trinkst.

Zum Glück hast du viele Möglichkeiten. Schließe dich einer Nüchternheitsgruppe oder einer Sportgruppe an, gehe zu einem Therapeuten, einem Coach oder einem Psychologen. Tue einfach etwas, das dich von deinen alten Gewohnheiten wegbringt.

Die Teilnahme an einer Gruppe kann dir bei vielen Dingen, die in diesem Buch bereits besprochen wurden, enorm helfen, z. B. beim aktiven Zuhören und beim Verstehen der

Gefühle anderer. Noch besser ist, dass du dort gleichgesinnte, nüchterne und authentische neue Freunde triffst.

Du kannst unserer eigenen Gruppe „Sober on a Drunk Planet" beitreten, indem du www.soberonadrunkplanet.com/community besuchst. Wir werden dich gerne auf deinem Weg unterstützen. Die Gruppe ist voll von Menschen, die den Weg bereits gegangen sind und die Nüchternheit „auf der anderen Seite" erlebt haben. In der Gruppe gibt es viele verschiedene Menschen mit unterschiedlichen Erfahrungen – und sie werden dir fast jede Frage beantworten können.

Deine **Selbstwahrnehmung**, dass du bessere Ergebnisse erzielst, wenn du von jemandem, etwas oder einer Gruppe zur Rechenschaft gezogen wirst, sollte dich dazu ermutigen, **positive Maßnahmen** zu ergreifen und auch dafür sorgen, dass du wirklich Ergebnisse erreichst. Außerdem macht es mehr Spaß!

Durch die Nutzung von Therapien, Nüchternheits-Apps und die Teilnahme an Nüchternheitsgruppen wirst du herausfinden, welche Gruppen funktionieren und welche nicht, und du wirst selektiver nach Gruppen sein, die dir Energie geben und dich wachsen lassen. Das ist die Entwicklung von **Intuition**.

***

Du bist jetzt mit einer Reihe von Strategien ausgerüstet, um deine Nüchternheit zu stärken. Im nächsten Kapitel sprechen wir über eine weitere Strategie: wie du deinen Körper und deinen Geist dazu bringst, richtig zusammenzuarbeiten – das *erleichtert* alles.

KAPITEL 7:

STARKER KÖRPER = STARKER GEIST. DIE BEDEUTUNG VON BEWEGUNG UND ERNÄHRUNG FÜR DEINE NÜCHTERNHEIT

Bewegung und Ernährung sind von grundlegender Bedeutung für die Gesundheit von Körper und Geist, wobei die Art und Weise, wie uns diese Dinge präsentiert werden, deprimierend eindimensional ist.

Fernsehwerbung und Marketingkampagnen scheinen sich immer darauf zu konzentrieren, Gewicht zu verlieren und Muskeln zuzulegen. Sie deuten eine einfache Gleichung an: Wenn du Sport treibst und dich gesund ernährst, wirst du gut aussehen. Und wenn du gut aussiehst, werden dich die Leute mögen und bewundern.

So einfach ist es aber nicht. Diese Kampagnen spielen direkt mit dem Ego – und wir haben bereits darüber gesprochen, wie das Ego funktioniert!

Das Problem mit diesem simplen Fokus auf Bewegung und Ernährung ist, dass er die vielen anderen lebensverbessernden Vorteile überspringt. Viele davon sind entscheidend, um eine stabile Nüchternheit aufzubauen und einen Rückfall zu vermeiden – deshalb konzentrieren wir uns in diesem Kapitel darauf.

Alkohol ist ein Gift. Er ist nicht im Entferntesten nahrhaft. Er schädigt aktiv den Mund, den Rachen, die Speiseröhre, den Magen, die Leber und den Darm. Ein einmaliges Trinken reicht aus, um „die Schleimhautzellen im Magen zu schädigen und Entzündungen und Läsionen hervorzurufen".

Schrecklich.

Alkoholkonsum ist auch ein zuverlässiger Weg, um jedes Sportprogramm zu gefährden, das du versuchst einzuhalten. Der Kater sorgt dafür, dass die meisten Läufe, Workouts und Sportkurse zu verworfenen guten Vorsätzen werden. Und dann setzt die negative Rückkopplungsschleife ein: Lethargie, fehlende

Motivation und ein Kreislauf der Scham, der direkt in die Kneipe führt.

Der Schaden, den Alkohol deiner Gesundheit zufügt

Lass uns einen Blick darauf werfen, auf welch erschreckende Weise Alkohol die Gesundheit von „chronisch Trinkenden" schädigt. Bevor wir damit anfangen, sollten wir den Begriff definieren. Bei dem Begriff „chronisch Trinkende" denkst du vielleicht an einen obdachlosen Alkoholiker, der jeden Tag mit einer Dose Spezialgebräu startet. Das ist aber nicht ganz richtig. Der Begriff bezieht sich auf alle, die mehr als 14 Einheiten Alkohol pro Woche trinken und nicht regelmäßig alkoholfreie Tage einlegen.[34]

VIELE Menschen sind chronische Trinkendende, ohne es zu merken oder es sich einzugestehen.

Hier sind einige der Schäden, die das Trinken verursacht:

- Alkohol stört die effektive Verarbeitung einer ganzen Reihe von Nährstoffen. Dazu gehören die Vitamine A, B, C, D, E und K, Mineralstoffe wie Magnesium,

Kalzium und Zink sowie Omega-3 Fettsäuren.

Wir brauchen ausreichend Vitamine und Mineralstoffe, um unser Immunsystem zu stärken, Zellen und Organe bei ihrer Arbeit zu unterstützen und ein normales Wachstum sowie für eine normale Entwicklung zu sorgen.

Sie sind also unverzichtbar.

- Alkohol schädigt den Darm und verursacht Krankheiten wie Darmdurchlässigkeit (Leaky Gut), Reizdarmsyndrom (IBS) und eine Überbesiedelung mit Bakterien. Dies kann schon bei „mäßigem Alkoholkonsum" auftreten. Die Liste der damit verbundenen Symptome umfasst Verstopfung, Durchfall, Blähungen, Müdigkeit, Angstzustände, Schmerzen und gedrückte Stimmung.

Ist es da verwunderlich, dass es Trinkenden schwerfällt, Sport zu treiben?

- Alkohol bringt deine Gehirnchemie ins Schleudern. Er bringt unter anderem Dopamin (das „Wohlfühlhormon"), Serotonin (den Neurotransmitter, der deine Stimmung reguliert) und GABA

(eine Aminosäure, die Stress und Angstzustände kontrolliert) durcheinander.
Mit all diesen Dingen solltest du dich nicht anlegen.

- Alkohol bringt die Hormone durcheinander und stört das Immun-, Nerven- und Hormonsystem. Das kann zu Problemen mit dem Adrenalinspiegel sowie zu Stimmungsschwankungen und Schlafproblemen führen.

Und wir haben noch gar nicht darüber gesprochen, was Alkohol der Leber antun kann.

Zu den alkoholbedingten Lebererkrankungen gehören die alkoholische Leberverfettung, die Alkoholhepatitis und die Leberzirrhose. Leider sind das alles auch keine angenehmen Folgen!

Ernährung und Bewegung sind zwei Seiten der gleichen Medaille. Es ist wichtig, beides in den Griff zu bekommen. Entgegen der landläufigen Meinung kannst du nicht essen, was du willst, und zum Ausgleich Sport treiben. Bei der Auswahl deiner Lebensmittel geht es um weit mehr als nur um die verbrauchten Kalorien.

So tröstlich es auch sein mag, diesem Mythos Glauben zu schenken, er ist genauso sinnvoll wie der Glaube, dass du dich so viel betrinken kannst, wie du willst, ohne einen Kater zu bekommen, solange du vor dem Schlafengehen zwei Gläser Wasser trinkst. Es stimmt einfach nicht.

Wer sich die Mühe gemacht hat, auf Alkohol zu verzichten, gibt sich leicht der Illusion hin, dass sich alles andere von selbst regeln wird.

Das ist nicht der Fall – und ich bin in diese Falle getappt.

Als ich aufhörte, Alkohol und Kokain zu mir zu nehmen, sehnte sich mein Körper nach Zucker. Unmengen von Zucker. Zucker macht süchtig und ist ein wesentlicher Bestandteil der meisten alkoholischen Getränke, die ich früher konsumierte.

Zucker erzeugt massive Dopaminschübe, genau wie Alkohol und Drogen. Er kann zu einer Kreuzabhängigkeit werden, und davor solltest du dich hüten. Auf Zucker werde ich gleich zurückkommen.

In nüchternen Communities rechtfertigen Menschen übermäßiges Essen oft damit, dass es „nicht so schlimm wie Alkoholkonsum" sei. Das geht an der Sache vorbei. Eine Sucht durch eine andere zu ersetzen, sollte nicht das Ziel sein. Erinnere dich daran, was wir zuvor in diesem Buch über das Gefühl gesagt haben, „reizbar, ruhelos und unzufrieden" zu sein?"

Ziel ist es, dieses Gefühl zu beseitigen - und nicht nur neue Wege zu finden, um es vorübergehend zu verdrängen.

Lebensverändernde Vorteile von Bewegung für die Nüchternheit

Als Personal Trainer empfehle ich dir dringend, mit Sport und Fitness zu starten. Es kann eine der lohnendsten Aktivitäten in der Nüchternheit werden. Sport kann deine Wochenenden ausfüllen, dir einen Grund geben, morgens aufzustehen, und dich daran gewöhnen, auf Ziele hinzuarbeiten.

Fit zu werden bringt eine ganze Reihe an Vorteilen mit sich, die dein Leben verändern und zu deiner dauerhaften Nüchternheit beitragen. Hier sind einige davon:

- Sport steigert dein Energielevel, indem er die Menge an Sauerstoff erhöht, die du einatmest – was durch den Wert VO2 Max gemessen wird.[35] Wenn du mehr Sauerstoff einatmest, hast du mehr

Energie zur Verfügung und weniger Energie möchte niemand haben!
Der VO2 Max-Wert wird von Sportlern verwendet, um ihr allgemeines Fitnesslevel zu bewerten. Du musst kein Sportler sein, um ihn zu messen oder ihn zu verbessern. Schon ein täglicher Spaziergang hilft.

- Regelmäßige körperliche Aktivität verbessert die Insulinempfindlichkeit.[36] Das hilft dem Körper, seinen Zuckerspiegel zu kontrollieren, was den Heißhunger reduziert. Warum das so wichtig ist, wirst du gleich sehen.

- Sport setzt Endorphine frei, die die Stimmung verbessern und Stress abbauen. (Ich habe noch *nie* erlebt, dass ein Klient nach einem Training zu mir kam und sagte, dass er es nicht genossen hat!)
Endorphine sind wichtig für die Nüchternheit – die positive Verstärkung dessen, dass du keinen Alkohol brauchst, um Momente purer Freude zu erleben, ist ungefähr so, als würdest du deinen Welpen zum ersten Mal draußen sein Geschäft erledigen sehen (und nicht wieder auf den Wohnzimmerteppich!). Es ist eine Verknüpfung von Verhalten und

Belohnung, die du immer wieder wiederholen möchtest. Es verstärkt die positiven Kreisläufe.

Außerdem ist das natürliche Hochgefühl nicht mit dem negativen Teufelskreis von Kater > bedauern > wiederholen verbunden, der uns unglücklich macht.

- Regelmäßige Bewegung kann dazu beitragen, den Teil unseres Gehirns zu verbessern, der für die Regulierung unserer Emotionen zuständig ist. Das wiederum hilft, Rückfälle zu verhindern, wie im Kapitel zur Regulierung von Emotionen beschrieben.

  Anstatt deine Wut an jemandem auszulassen, empfehle ich einen Muay Thai-Kurs oder eine Runde Hot Yoga. Danach *wirst du nicht mehr* die gleichen Emotionen in dir tragen wie zuvor. Du wirst sehen, wie die Regulierung der Emotionen funktioniert.

- Bewegung bringt das Blut im Körper zum Fließen. Das verbessert die Leber- und Nierenfunktion [37] und hilft dem Körper, Giftstoffe auszuscheiden. Entgegen der landläufigen Meinung kannst du sie nicht einfach „ausschwitzen"!

- Sport (und eine gesunde Ernährung) können helfen, eine Fettlebererkrankung zu überwinden. [38]

- Sport hilft dir, natürliches Selbstvertrauen aufzubauen. Es stimmt zwar, dass ein schlankeres, kräftigeres und jüngeres Aussehen dein Ego beeinflusst, aber es lässt sich auch nicht leugnen, dass das etwas ist, was alle wollen! Wenn du selbstbewusster bist, fühlst du dich in sozialen Situationen wohler. Das bedeutet, dass du viel seltener Alkohol trinkst, um dein Unbehagen zu lindern.

- Die Wissenschaft beweist, dass Sport deine kognitiven Funktionen und deine Fähigkeit, Probleme zu lösen, verbessert.[39] Ein nüchternes Leben zu führen bedeutet, immer wieder die richtigen Entscheidungen zu treffen und die besten Maßnahmen zu wählen. Ein klarer Kopf hilft dabei!

- Bewegung macht dich körperlich stärker. Die Menschen unterschätzen oft den Unterschied, den es ausmacht, funktionell stark zu sein – nicht mehr vor Anstrengung stöhnen zu müssen, wenn man etwas aufhebt oder einen Schnürsenkel zubindet!

Wenn du trinkst, kannst du träge werden und an Muskelmasse und Knochendichte verlieren. Kraft- und Widerstandstraining kann das wieder rückgängig machen und dir zeigen, dass du Muskeln hast, von denen du gar nicht wusstest, dass du sie hast!

- Die Entwicklung von Fähigkeiten, das Überwinden von Schmerzgrenzen und das Übertreffen persönlicher Bestleistungen helfen dabei, körperliche und geistige Widerstandsfähigkeit aufzubauen. Du gehst in jede Trainingseinheit und treibst dich selbst an, um es jedes Mal um 1 % besser zu machen. Das ist das wichtigste Prinzip, um fitter und stärker zu werden – progressives Überlasten. Du kannst dieses Prinzip auch in allen anderen Bereichen des Lebens anwenden.

- Bewegung kann dir helfen, Schlaflosigkeit zu besiegen und deine Schlafqualität zu verbessern.[40] Ich kann gar nicht genug betonen, wie wichtig es ist, regelmäßig sieben oder acht Stunden erholsamen Schlaf zu bekommen.
Alkohol stört den Schlaf ohnehin erheblich. Starker Alkoholkonsum verringert die Schlafqualität um 39,2 %

und kann auch die Schlafapnoe verschlimmern.[41]

Guter Schlaf setzt einen eigenen positiven Kreislauf in Gang. Wenn du ausgeruht aufwachst, ist die Wahrscheinlichkeit größer, dass du mehr Sport treibst und dich gesünder ernährst (anstatt müde einen Imbiss zu bestellen und auf dem Sofa zusammenzubrechen).

- Es ist medizinisch erwiesen, dass regelmäßiger Sport das Risiko für koronare Herzkrankheiten, Schlaganfall, Typ-2-Diabetes, Darmkrebs, Brustkrebs, frühen Tod, Arthrose, Depressionen und Demenz senkt.[42] Das ist schon eine ziemlich lange Liste.
- Bewegung (insbesondere Yoga) kann dir helfen, deine Reaktion auf vergangene Traumata zu überwinden und zu bewältigen.[43]

Das könnte ich noch weiter fortsetzten.

Bewegung ist wirklich Medizin und geht weit über das Abnehmen und den Muskelaufbau hinaus.

Es gibt überall Möglichkeiten, sich zu bewegen. Also gibt es keine Ausreden! (Falls dir doch welche einfallen, lohnt es sich, den Abschnitt über limitierende Glaubenssätze im vorherigen Kapitel noch einmal zu lesen).

Also geh ins Fitnessstudio, besuche einen Kurs, gehe spazieren, schließe dich einem Sportverein an, lade dir eine Trainings-App herunter oder suche dir ein paar Yoga-Videos auf YouTube. Tue, was auch immer nötig ist, um deine Herzfrequenz und deine Lungen in Schwung zu bringen.

Wenn du das nötige Budget hast, kannst du ein Personal Trainer oder ein Kraft- und Konditionstrainer engagieren, um deine Ziele zu erreichen. Das Training in der Gruppe ist eine weitere Option, bei der du dich gegenüber anderen Gruppenmitgliedern verpflichtest.

Denke daran, wie wichtig positives Handeln ist. Bereite deine Trainingskleidung vor und stelle dir am Abend vorher einen Wecker. Verpflichte dich, und sorge dafür, dass du den ersten Schritt machst.

Wenn Leute sagen, dass es am schwierigsten ist, den Hintern von der Couch zu heben, dann stimmt das. Genauso wie niemand bereut, nüchtern geworden zu sein, bereut auch niemand, Sport getrieben zu haben (es sei denn, er hat versucht, mit einem Kater zu trainieren!).

Denke auch daran, dass Motivation durch Handeln entsteht. Positives Handeln zieht *mehr* positives Handeln nach sich.

So wie Alkohol der Treibstoff für die negativen Kreisläufe war, kann Bewegung der Treibstoff für die positiven Kreisläufe sein. Sie kann dich auch dabei unterstützen, dich in der Nüchternheit weiterzuentwickeln und dich wohlzufühlen.

Ernährung und die Stärke deines Darms

Wie bereits erwähnt, ist Bewegung nur ein Teil der Gleichung. Schauen wir uns an, wie die Ernährung dazu beitragen kann, dass du nüchtern bleibst.

Eine ausgewogene Ernährung hat folgende Auswirkungen:

- Sie trägt dazu bei, dass du besser schläfst. Neben vielen anderen Vorteilen hilft mehr Schlaf bei der Insulinsensitivität (die mit Heißhunger zusammenhängt) und trägt dazu bei, deine Gefühle besser zu regulieren. Du brauchst nur einmal schlecht zu schlafen, um zu verstehen, wie schrecklich du dich am nächsten Tag fühlst und in welche Stimmung dich das versetzt.

- Sie stabilisiert deinen Blutzuckerspiegel, gleicht deine Stimmung aus und reduziert Heißhungerattacken.

- Sie nährt deine Leber und hilft dabei, deinen Körper zu entgiften (das Gegenteil von dem, was Alkohol bewirkt!).

- Sie unterstützt die effektive Funktion der Neurotransmitter, die eine wichtige Rolle bei der Weiterleitung chemischer Signale spielen, die unsere Stimmung, unseren Schlafzyklus, unsere Verdauung und unsere Herzfrequenz steuern.

- Sie gleicht Defizite im Bereich der Mikro- und Makronährstoffe aus. Wenn wir zum Beispiel nicht genügend Eisen zu uns nehmen, können wir an Anämie leiden, was zu Müdigkeit führt. Wenn wir uns schwächer fühlen, sinkt unsere Widerstandskraft und wir werden anfälliger für schlechte Entscheidungen, z. B. wenn wir nachgeben und etwas trinken.

- Sie unterstützt die Gesundheit des Darms, damit wir wichtige Nährstoffe aus der Nahrung aufnehmen können. Wenn wir die Nährstoffe, die unser Körper braucht, nicht effizient aufnehmen können, kann es zu Mangelerscheinungen und Krankheiten kommen, die sich auf unsere Stimmung auswirken und dazu führen können, dass wir wieder auf den großen roten Knopf drücken.

Sowohl die Darmgesundheit als auch die Darm-Hirn-Achse habe ich schon ein paar Mal erwähnt. Hier ist der Grund, warum sie so wichtig sind:

Wenn Menschen von einem „Bauchgefühl" sprechen, ist das mehr als nur ein Spruch. Der Darm ist – wissenschaftlich gesehen – unser zweites Gehirn. Man könnte sogar behaupten, dass es unser primäres Gehirn ist. Das liegt daran, dass mehr Nerven vom Darm zum Gehirn führen als umgekehrt.

Die Natur hat hier eine klare Botschaft: Achte auf deinen Darm!

Als ich stark getrunken habe, war es um meine Darmgesundheit furchtbar bestellt. Viele Jahre lang litt ich unter dem Reizdarmsyndrom und saurem Reflux – bis ich endlich begann, die Darmgesundheit zu verstehen. Als ich mir des Problems bewusst wurde, habe ich meine Ernährung umgestellt. Im Ergebnis musste ich nicht mehr in der Angst leben, es nicht rechtzeitig auf die nächste Toilette zu schaffen!

In deinem Darm – und auch im Rest deines Körpers – wimmelt es von Bakterien und Pilzen. Das klingt ziemlich eklig, aber das meiste davon spielt eine entscheidende Rolle bei der Erhaltung von Gesundheit und Leben. Von diesen Zellen gibt es sogar mehr auf und in deinem Körper als menschliche Zellen.[44]

Wenn du deine Darmgesundheit auf Vordermann bringst, kann das Folgendes bewirken:

- Du verhinderst eine Darmdysbiose, d.h. ein Ungleichgewicht der Darmbakterien, das u.a. zu Gewichtszunahme, Müdigkeit, Hauterkrankungen, Angstzuständen, Depressionen und Konzentrationsproblemen führen kann.[45]
- Du verbesserst deine Herzgesundheit, indem du das „gute" HDL-Cholesterin und die Triglyceride ankurbelst.[46] Das ist wichtig, um Herzinfarkte und Schlaganfälle zu vermeiden.
- Du senkst deinen Blutzucker und dein Diabetes-Risiko.[47]

- Du reduzierst die Entzündungen in deinem Körper. Entzündungen können zahlreiche Krankheiten verursachen, darunter entzündliche Darmerkrankungen, rheumatoide Arthritis und Schuppenflechte. Zudem sind sie „ein wesentlicher Faktor für Krankheiten wie Krebs, Diabetes und Herz-Kreislauf-Erkrankungen".[48]
- Du linderst Leaky Gut, Reizdarmsyndrom und sauren Reflux und verhinderst, dass sich krankmachende Bakterien an den Darmwänden festsetzen. (Bifidobakterien und Laktobazillen, die in Probiotika und Joghurt enthalten sind, sollen dabei helfen.)[49]

In den letzten zehn Jahren sind immer mehr Forschungsergebnisse aufgetaucht, die zeigen, wie stark die Beziehung zwischen Darm und Gehirn tatsächlich ist.

„Die Darm-Hirn-Achse (GBA) besteht aus einer bidirektionalen Kommunikation zwischen dem zentralen und dem enterischen Nervensystem, die emotionale und kognitive Zentren des Gehirns mit peripheren Darmfunktionen verbindet. Jüngste Fortschritte in der Forschung haben die Bedeutung der Darmmikrobiota bei der Beeinflussung dieser Interaktionen beschrieben."[50]

Im Klartext bedeutet das, dass die Art und Weise, wie wir unseren Bauch behandeln, einen RIESIGEN Einfluss darauf hat, wie wir uns fühlen. Wie wir uns fühlen, wirkt sich direkt auf unsere Handlungen aus. Eine gute Darmgesundheit trägt also zu einer dauerhaften Nüchternheit bei. Ohne eine gute Darmgesundheit riskierst du schlechte Laune, Angstzustände und Stress. All diese Faktoren erhöhen die Wahrscheinlichkeit eines Rückfalls.

Intuition ist nicht nur eine Sache des Gehirns – sie ist auch eine Sache des Bauches.

Der Vagusnerv verbindet das Gehirn und den Darm. Eine Kombination aus Bewegung und gesunder Ernährung trägt dazu bei, den Vagustonus zu verbessern. Dies führt zu all den Vorteilen, die wir gerade besprochen haben.

Wir haben viel über Intuition gesprochen. Intuition ist ein *Bauchgefühl*. Sie interagiert mit unterbewussten Gedanken. Der Schlüssel zu einer dauerhaften Veränderung des Lebensstils liegt darin, dafür zu sorgen, dass der Darm gut genährt wird – mit den richtigen Lebensmitteln und einem guten Gleichgewicht an Bakterien.

Ein Darm, der Alkohol verarbeiten muss, ist KEIN gut genährter Darm!

So startest du mit deiner Ernährung und deinem Darm-Biom

Ernährung kann unglaublich komplex sein und hängt von deinen eigenen Lebensumständen ab. Wenn du die finanziellen Mittel hast, solltest du in Erwägung ziehen, mit einem Ernährungsberater zu arbeiten. Das ist eine großartige Möglichkeit, deine Selbstwahrnehmung zu stärken und gleichzeitig eine gewisse Verantwortung zu übernehmen, während du auf das Ziel hinarbeitest, deine Ernährung zu verbessern.

Das ist aber nicht unbedingt notwendig. Du kannst auch Bücher über Ernährung lesen, Kurse besuchen oder neugierig werden und selbstbewusst wahrnehmen, was du deinem Körper zuführst. So wirst du schon bald die Zusammenhänge erkennen und bessere Entscheidungen bei der Ernährung treffen.

Hier ist eine gute Möglichkeit, damit anzufangen: Frage dich, wie du dich nach jeder Mahlzeit fühlst. Fühlst du dich energiegeladen und angenehm satt oder fühlst du dich lethargisch und träge? Du wirst schnell merken, welche Lebensmittel dir Energie geben und welche dich einschränken.

Um einen gesunden Darm aufzubauen, ist es wichtig zu wissen, wie man die *guten* Bakterien gedeihen lässt. Werfen wir also einen Blick auf Prä- und Probiotika.

Präbiotika sind spezielle Pflanzenfasern, die Bakterien das Wachstum ermöglichen. Du kannst ihn dir wie den Kompost vorstellen, den du brauchst, um eine blühende Pflanze wachsen zu lassen - es geht darum, eine gesunde Grundlage zu schaffen. Obst, Gemüse, Hafer, Vollkorn und Getreide sind allesamt gute Quellen für Präbiotika.

Probiotika sind die lebenden Bakterien und Hefen, die in unserem Darm wachsen. Es gibt viele Nahrungsergänzungsmittel und probiotische Joghurts, die diese „guten Bakterien" enthalten und angeblich zur allgemeinen Darmgesundheit beitragen.

Weitere natürliche Quellen für Probiotika sind Kefir, Sauerkraut, Kimchi, Miso und Kombucha. Ich habe die meisten dieser Produkte ausprobiert und ich mochte sie alle. Allerdings kann bei der Fermentierung einiger dieser Produkte ein extrem niedriger Alkoholgehalt entstehen, der Teil des Prozesses ist. Je nachdem, wie du zu Alkohol in Lebensmitteln und Gesundheitsgetränken stehst, solltest du die Verpackung überprüfen. Wenn vorhanden, sollte auf der Verpackung der Alkoholgehalt angegeben sein.

Zusammen mit der Bewegung verbessert die Kultivierung guter Bakterien in unserem Magen unseren gesamten Vagustonus. Das hat einen enormen Einfluss auf unsere Stimmung, unseren Stress und unsere Angst. Wenn wir ein Stimmungstief vermeiden wollen, liegt der Schlüssel darin, das Gleichgewicht zu halten.

Wenn du deinen Darm nicht mit einem gesunden Gleichgewicht an nahrhaften Lebensmitteln fütterst, die es guten Bakterien ermöglichen, zu gedeihen und zu wachsen, kann das deine Fähigkeit, deine Intuition aufzubauen, ernsthaft beeinträchtigen. Wenn du ständig Lebensmittel zu dir nimmst, die dich in ein Stimmungstief versetzen - wie z. B. zuckerhaltige Lebensmittel mit geringem oder gar keinem Nährwert – bist du deutlich gefährdeter, rückfällig zu werden.

Bei einem Stück Schokolade am Abend sagt niemand etwas – aber wenn du ignorierst, was du deinem Körper zuführst, begibst du dich möglicherweise auf einen gefährlichen Pfad.

Menschen mit einer guten Intuition ernähren sich in der Regel nicht von Fertiggerichten, Süßigkeiten und Schokolade!

Und damit sind wir wieder beim Zucker.

Das Problem mit Zucker und Rückfällen

Zucker und Alkoholabhängigkeit sind eng miteinander verbunden.

Ein Glas Cider kann bis zu fünf Teelöffel Zucker enthalten – fast so viel wie die empfohlene Tagesmenge für Erwachsene.[51] Es ist also nicht schwer zu verstehen, dass wir, wenn wir unser Lieblingsgetränk aufgeben, genauso unter Zuckerentzug leiden können wie unter Alkoholentzug.

Ich habe früher an einem Abend 10 Gläser Cider getrunken. Das sind 250 Gramm Zucker – mehr als das Achtfache der empfohlenen Tagesmenge. Und da ist noch nicht einmal der Zucker berücksichtigt, den ich in dieser Zeit in anderen Getränken und Lebensmitteln zu mir genommen habe.

Die Zuckerarten, die wir berücksichtigen sollten, sind „freie Zucker". Dazu gehören:

- Alle Zuckerarten, die Lebensmitteln oder Getränken zugesetzt werden. Dazu gehören Zucker in Keksen, Schokolade, aromatisierten Joghurts, Frühstücksflocken und kohlensäurehaltigen Getränken. Dieser Zucker kann zu Hause oder von einem Koch oder Lebensmittelhersteller hinzugefügt werden.
- Zucker in Honig, Sirup (z. B. Ahornsirup und goldener Sirup), Nektar (z. B. Blütennektar) und „ungesüßten" Fruchtsäften, Gemüsesäften und Smoothies. Der Zucker in diesen Lebensmitteln kommt natürlich vor, zählt aber trotzdem zu den freien Zuckern.

Zu viel Zucker kann zu Hypoglykämie führen. Eine Unterzuckerung wird als „metabolische Achterbahn" beschrieben [52] "und ist der Inbegriff einer negativen Rückkopplungsschleife für Körper und Geist.

Der Konsum von Zucker (oder Alkohol) erzeugt ein kurzes Hochgefühl. Dann produziert der Körper Insulin, woraufhin der Blutzuckerspiegel sinkt, die Stimmung sinkt und es fehlt an

Energie. Als Nächstes produziert der Körper Adrenalin, und damit kommen Heißhunger und Angst, die in der Regel durch den Konsum von mehr Zucker (oder Alkohol) in die Flucht geschlagen werden.

Mit der Zeit wird der Körper adrenalinmüde. Er ist weniger in der Lage, Adrenalin zu produzieren und wird resistenter gegen Insulin. Infolgedessen steigt und fällt der Blutdruck wie ein Jo-Jo, der Stoffwechsel verlangsamt sich und du bist im endlosen Kreislauf des Heißhungers gefangen.

Ein hypoglykämischer Alkoholiker braucht nicht nur Alkohol, damit sich seine Gehirnchemie „normal" anfühlt. Er führt auch einen endlosen Kampf mit seinem Blutzuckerspiegel. Das macht den Heißhunger extrem und alles verzehrend.

Wie viel Zucker du konsumierst, ist von großer Bedeutung – vor allem, wenn du aufhörst zu trinken. Dann läufst du Gefahr, das Verlangen nach Zucker mit dem Verlangen nach Alkohol zu verwechseln.

Natürlich kannst du einen Kuchen, ein Softdrink oder ein Eis genießen. Aber es wird dir gut tun, wenn du lernst, den Heißhunger auf Zucker in den Griff zu bekommen.

So besiegst du den Heißhunger auf Zucker

Hier sind einige Tipps, die dir helfen, Heißhunger auf Zucker zu vermeiden, wenn du Trinken aufgibst:

- Aus den Augen, aus dem Sinn. Wenn du also weißt, dass etwas nicht gut für dich ist, solltest du es nicht auf Vorrat im Küchenschrank haben.
- Plane im Voraus und überlege dir für jede Mahlzeit, was du essen möchtest. So verhinderst du, dass du zu etwas Ungesundem greifst, wenn du hungrig bist.
- Iss mehr Eiweiß – das hilft dir, dich satt zu fühlen.
- Iss regelmäßig ein Frühstück, das viele Ballaststoffe, aber wenig Zucker enthält (z. B. Vollkornmüsli oder Porridge). Ein Hinweis: Die meisten Müslis und Müsliriegel sehen zwar gesund aus, enthalten aber sehr viel Zucker. Das kann dazu führen, dass du den ganzen Tag über naschen musst - also überprüfe die Angaben auf dem Etikett, bevor du die Produkte kaufst.

- Versuche, jede Nacht acht Stunden zu schlafen. Passe deine Routine an, damit das funktioniert.

- Achte darauf, dein Stressniveau zu senken. Stress setzt mehr Cortisol in deinem Körper frei, was zu Heißhunger führt. Meditation, Yoga, Sport und eine ganze Reihe anderer Aktivitäten können helfen, Stress abzubauen.

- Gewöhne dir an, die Etiketten von Lebensmitteln zu lesen. Dadurch steigt deine Selbstwahrnehmung für das, was du isst. **Selbstwahrnehmung** (was sagt mir dieses Etikett?) > **Positives Handeln** (gesünder essen) > **Intuition** (du weißt, wie du dich nach dem Verzehr dieses bestimmten Lebensmittels fühlst).

- Nutze Ablenkungsmethoden, um deinen Mund zu beschäftigen. Kaue zum Beispiel zuckerfreies Kaugummi, trinke Kräutertee oder benutze einfach einen Zahnstocher!

- Wenn du gerne Süßes isst, ziehe das Natürliche dem Verarbeiteten vor - iss Obst und dunkle Schokolade statt Süßigkeiten und Kekse.

- Arbeite daran, intuitiver zu essen. Reflektiere, wie sich alles, was du isst, auf dich auswirkt. Hilft es dir oder hindert es dich eher?

- Mach dich damit vertraut, dass du dich unwohl fühlst. Nimm das unangenehme Verlangen nach Zucker hin, widerstehe weiter und beobachte, wie du dich fühlst. Das Verlangen wird vergehen!

Eine weitere gute Übung ist es, eine Woche lang ein Zuckertagebuch zu führen. Jedes Mal, wenn du das Verlangen nach etwas Süßem hast, schreibst du auf, was es war, wann du es wolltest und in welchem Zusammenhang. Hattest du zum Beispiel direkt nach dem Abendessen Lust auf etwas Süßes oder kurz vor deiner Lieblingssendung? Warum hast du nach dem Snack gegriffen? Warst du genervt?

Das hilft dir, deine Selbstwahrnehmung in Bezug auf den gewohnheitsmäßigen Verzehr von Zucker zu schärfen, und gibt dir die Zeit und den Raum, eine andere Entscheidung zu treffen (weil sie dir bewusst geworden ist und nicht mehr nur eine unterbewusste Reaktion ist).

Dann ergreifst du positive Maßnahmen (indem du eine Alternative zum Zucker findest). Wenn du die Früchte des Zuckerverzichts oder der Zuckerreduzierung erntest, entwickelt sich mit der Zeit eine gesündere Intuition. Es dreht sich alles um die Belohnung – der gleiche Mechanismus wie bei Alkohol.

Der Drei-Schritte-Prozess kann für alles verwendet werden, was du verbessern willst, egal ob es darum geht, mit Alkohol, Zucker oder etwas anderem aufzuhören.

Ähnlich wie bei der Alkoholentwöhnung ist es gut, sich nicht darauf zu konzentrieren, was du „aufgibst", sondern auf das, was du zurückbekommst.

Bei Zucker ist es nicht notwendig, einen „kalten Entzug" zu machen. Aber es ist gut, darauf zu achten, wie du dem Heißhunger auf Zucker begegnen kannst, während du auf Alkohol verzichtest. Freier Zucker hat so gut wie keinen Nutzen für die Gesundheit. Alles, was du aufgibst, ist eine Gewichtszunahme (mit den damit verbundenen gesundheitlichen Problemen) sowie ein ständiges „Auf und Ab".

***

Bewegung und eine gute Ernährung sind mächtige Werkzeuge, um nüchtern bleiben zu können und widerstandsfähiger werden. Sie haben auch den erwünschten Nebeneffekt, dass sie lebensbedrohlichen Krankheiten vorbeugen.

Sich gesund zu ernähren und fit zu bleiben, ist ein positiver Kreislauf, der deine Intuition weiter stärkt.

Es ist viel Wahres an dem Ausspruch, dass die Qualität deines Lebens von der Qualität deiner Gedanken abhängt. Aber die Qualität deiner Gedanken hängt auch davon ab, wie du deinen Körper ernährst – durch Bewegung und durch das, was du isst.

Die Darm-Hirn-Achse zeigt das besonders gut.

Wenn du dich gesund ernährst und mehr bewegst, stärkst du deine **Selbstwahrnehmung**, damit du dich gesünder und glücklicher fühlst. Das lässt sich nicht leugnen. Diese positiven Gefühle fördern positive Gedanken – und diese wiederum fördern **positive Handlungen**.

Das Ergebnis dieser positiven Kreisläufe besteht darin, dass du dir einer unbestreitbaren Tatsache bewusst wirst: Wie sich dein Geist fühlt, hängt direkt damit zusammen, wie du deinen Körper behandelst. Je mehr du das in deinem Unterbewusstsein verinnerlichst, desto mehr entwickelst du deine **Intuition**.

Wenn du das nächste Mal trainierst, nimm dir die Zeit, dir bewusst zu machen, wie du dich fühlst, bevor du anfängst und wie du dich 30 Minuten später fühlst. Hat sich deine Stimmung verändert? Ist dein Energielevel anders?

Wenn du das nächste Mal etwas Fett- und Zuckerhaltiges isst, z. B. eine Pizza, einen oder einen Snack im Kino, mache dasselbe. Wie fühlst du dich danach? Wie fühlst du dich am nächsten Tag? Empfindest du Scham oder Schuldgefühle wegen deiner Entscheidungen?

Je öfter du das tust, desto mehr wirst du anfangen, dich intuitiv zu ernähren und dir bewusst zu machen, wie sich Essen und Bewegung auf deine Stimmung, deinen Körper und deine Energie auswirken.

Mit dem Gedanken an Energie kommen wir zum letzten Kapitel. Gerade haben wir die Energie besprochen, die wir unserem Körper zuführen und durch Bewegung nutzen. Als Nächstes geht es darum, zu verstehen, wie die Schwingungsenergie die Nüchternheit beeinflusst.

KAPITEL 8:

VERKATERTE ENERGIE VS. NÜCHTERNE ENERGIE: SCHÜTZE DEINE ENERGIE UM JEDEN PREIS

Schwingungsenergie klingt vielleicht nach einem Thema, das man eher in der spirituellen Abteilung einer Buchhandlung finden würde. Aber es gibt immer mehr Belege dafür, dass die Schwingungsmedizin (oder Energiemedizin) allen, die ihre Gesundheit und ihr Wohlbefinden verbessern wollen, eine Menge zu bieten hat. Es ist entscheidend, das Konzept von Energie und ihrem Fluss zu verstehen, wenn du langfristig nüchtern bleiben möchtest.

Was ist Schwingungsenergie?

Der Mensch besteht aus energieproduzierenden Teilchen, die permanent in Bewegung sind. Wie alle anderen Menschen auf der Welt schwingen

222

wir und erzeugen Energie. Wir erzeugen sogar unser eigenes Energiefeld. Vermutlich ist das nichts, was du erfahren würdest, wenn du die meisten Wochenenden verkatert verbringst!

Die Konzepte von Schwingungen und dem Energiefluss sind bereits seit Jahrtausenden ein wichtiger Bestandteil aller möglichen Praktiken, die sich bei Millionen von Menschen großer Beliebtheit erfreuen. Sind die Menschen, die chinesische Medizin, Yoga, Chakren, Qigong, Feng Shui, Reiki, Klangheilung und Akupunktur praktizieren, also nur auf dem Holzweg und machen sich etwas vor? Das scheint kaum wahrscheinlich.

Rhythmen und Schwingungen sind überall. Im Wind, in den Gezeiten und sogar in einzelnen Molekülen, die mit unterschiedlichen Geschwindigkeiten schwingen, wenn sich das Wetter ändert. Auch im menschlichen Körper gibt es zahlreiche Rhythmen und Schwingungen – das Schlagen des Herzens, der zirkadiane Rhythmus oder Atemmuster.

Viele Rhythmen und Schwingungen können gemessen werden – Herzfrequenz und Blutdruck sind zwei Beispiele. Interessant ist zum Beispiel, dass es Wissenschaftlern gelungen ist, Schwingungen in Bereichen zu erkennen, die

„kleiner als 1/1000 des Durchmessers eines einzelnen menschlichen Haares sind". [53]

Diejenigen, die sich für das Bewusstsein der Schwingungsenergie einsetzen, gehen davon aus, dass „es möglich ist, die Schwingungen auf zellulärer und atomarer Ebene zu beschleunigen oder zu verlangsamen, indem wir unsere Gedanken, unser Verhalten – und sogar unsere Umgebung – verändern".

Falls du daran zweifelst, dass es sinnvoll sein kann, sich die Bedeutung der Schwingungsenergie bewusst zu machen, solltest du Folgendes bedenken:

- Wie dein Herz rast und dein Körper reagiert, wenn du denkst, dass du dein Portemonnaie oder deine Tasche im Zug vergessen hast, der gerade den Bahnhof verlassen hat.
- Wie du dich ständig müde und ausgelaugt fühlst, wenn du Zeit mit bestimmten Menschen verbringst.
- Wie das Hören des richtigen Liedes zur richtigen Zeit deine Stimmung verändern kann. (Töne und Musik werden durch Schwingungen erzeugt.)

- Wie du manchmal einen Raum betrittst und sofort eine negative Stimmung zwischen den Anwesenden wahrnehmen kannst.

Es scheint doch recht wahrscheinlich, dass wir so beschaffen sind, dass wir die Energie um uns herum wahrnehmen und absorbieren.

Die Theorie der Schwingungsenergie geht davon aus, dass manche Menschen, Orte, Gefühle und Dinge eine niedrige Schwingungsenergie haben können und andere eine hohe Schwingungsenergie. Es wird zum Beispiel angenommen, dass negative Emotionen wie Wut und Angst eine niedrigere Schwingung haben als Gefühle von Frieden und Freude.

Deshalb spielt Schwingungsenergie eine Rolle und so kannst du sie nutzen

Ziel ist es, dein Leben so zu gestalten, dass du viel gute (hohe) Energie aufnimmst und schlechte (niedrige) Energie vermeidest. Auch hier ist die Selbstwahrnehmung der Schlüssel. Je mehr du dir bewusst machst, wie verschiedene Menschen, Orte, Gefühle und Dinge deine Energie beeinflussen, desto mehr kannst du die richtigen Maßnahmen ergreifen, um das Leben zu gestalten, das du möchtest.

Stell dir vor, wie es sich anfühlt, verkatert zu sein. Das ist eine negative, schwache Energie.

Regelmäßig Trinkende sind oft „niedrigschwingend". Sie mögen nette Menschen sein, aber sie haben ihre eigenen Gründe für ihre Angewohnheiten – vielleicht ein ungelöstes Trauma oder eine allgemeine Unzufriedenheit mit ihrem Leben. (An dieser Stelle sei angemerkt, dass Alkohol niemanden in einen "High-Viber" verwandelt – er macht ihn nur betrunken!)

Betrachte im Gegensatz dazu eine Gruppe nüchterner Menschen nach einem Sportkurs, einer Wanderung oder einer Freizeitaktivität. Sie wirken glücklich und strahlen vor Energie. Sie sind „hochschwingend" – gut genährt, gut trainiert und nehmen positive Energie von Menschen mit einem gemeinsamen Interesse auf.

Das alles mag sich für dich wie spiritueller Humbug anhören. Glaub mir, es hat auch bei mir etwas gedauert, bis ich meine anfänglichen Vorbehalte überwunden hatte. Aber Tatsache ist, dass Menschen (auch du) gute oder schlechte

Energie aussenden. Was du in deinem täglichen Leben tust, wirkt sich positiv oder negativ auf diese Schwingungen aus. Letztendlich hast du die Kontrolle darüber.

Wenn du nüchtern bist, kannst du anfangen, dich und dein Energielevel wirklich zu verstehen. Du kannst herausfinden, welche Menschen, Orte, Gefühle und Dinge dir Auftrieb geben und welche dich runterziehen.

Positive Gefühle und Gedanken bringen dich in Hochstimmung. Mit anderen nüchternen Menschen zusammen zu sein, die daran arbeiten, eine bessere Version ihrer selbst zu werden, fühlt sich ganz anders an, als in einer Kneipe zu sitzen. Oft sind diese Orte voller Menschen, die sich über andere lustig machen und über ihr Schicksal jammern. (Ich weiß es, denn ich war einer von ihnen).

Wenn du deine positiven Kreisläufe anregen möchtest, ist es wichtig, dass du deine Zeit mit Menschen verbringst, die hohe Schwingungen haben – an Orten, die hohe Schwingungen haben, und mit Dingen, die hohe Schwingungen haben. Die meisten Ideen, die wir in diesem Buch erkundet haben, tragen ebenfalls dazu bei – positive Gedanken, Emotionen und ein gesunder Körper tragen alle zu einer höheren Schwingungsfrequenz bei.

Hier sind einige Möglichkeiten, deine Schwingungsfrequenz positiv zu beeinflussen:

- Verbringe Zeit mit positiven Menschen, die einen ähnlichen Weg der Selbstfindung und des persönlichen Wachstums gehen. Motivationsredner Jim Rohn sagt dazu: „Wir sind der Durchschnitt der fünf Menschen, mit denen wir die meiste Zeit verbringen."[54]
- Verbringe Zeit an positiven Orten: im Fitnessstudio, im Theater, im Kino, auf der Bowlingbahn, in der Bibliothek und bei Familie und Freunden, die dir ein gutes Gefühl geben. Verbringe deine Zeit nicht an Orten, die dich immer wieder an deiner Nüchternheit zweifeln lassen, wie Bars und Clubs!
- Bewege dich! Es klingt wie ein Widerspruch, aber du solltest dich regelmäßig bewegen, um dich energiegeladen zu fühlen. Wir haben ja bereits festgestellt, wie wichtig Bewegung ist, um deinem Körper mehr Energie zu liefern.

- Ernähre dich nährstoffreich. Die Energie, die du zu dir nimmst, ist genauso wichtig wie die Energie deiner Gedanken und Gefühle.

- Nutze Therapien, die den Energiefluss berücksichtigen, wie Reiki, Klangheilung und Yoga. Lass alle Vorurteile beiseite – und probiere es einfach aus. Du wirst überrascht sein, wie wirkungsvoll diese Aktivitäten sind, um Blockaden aufzulösen und dein Energielevel zu steigern.

- Verbringe so viel Zeit wie möglich in der Natur. Es gibt immer mehr wissenschaftliche Beweise für die Kraft der Erdung und der Rückverbindung mit der Erde. Studien zeigen, dass sich Müdigkeit, chronische Schmerzen, Angstzustände und sogar der Blutdruck positiv verändern.[55] Das ist die perfekte Ausrede, um mehr Golf zu spielen, an den Strand zu gehen oder den Baum zu umarmen, auf den du ein Auge geworfen hast!

- Mach nüchternen Urlaub. Das gibt dir die Möglichkeit, dich wirklich zu erholen. Dann bist du weit entfernt von den Urlauben, in denen du deinen Körper und

Geist noch mehr strapazierst als zu Hause!

- Arbeite daran, bei allem, was du tust, wirklich präsent und „im Moment" zu sein. Das ist ein guter Weg, um die Energie positiv zu kanalisieren. Du hast sicher schon viele Gespräche mit Leuten geführt, die mit dem Kopf nicken, obwohl du weißt, dass sie nicht wirklich zuhören. Gehöre nicht zu diesen Leuten.
- Vermeide „Energiediebe". Es gibt mit Sicherheit Menschen, die dich nach jedem Gespräch müde und ausgelaugt zurücklassen. Dieses Gefühl der Erschöpfung ist deine Selbstwahrnehmung - sie sagt dir, dass diese Menschen dir nicht gut tun. Verbringe also so wenig Zeit wie möglich mit Menschen, die dich so fühlen lassen.
- Sei enthusiastisch: Salsa tanzen, Kung Fu, Schallplatten sammeln, Berge besteigen – mach all das, was deine Seele zum Singen bringt und dir positive Energie gibt.

Wenn deine Gedanken, Gefühle und Handlungen im Einklang sind, wirst du dich besser denn je fühlen. Je mehr du deine **Selbstwahrnehmung** schärfst und **positive Maßnahmen** für dein eigenes Energielevel ergreifst, desto mehr werden diese Dinge **intuitiv**.

Du wirst intuitiv Einladungen zu Veranstaltungen ablehnen, bei denen du dich ausgelaugt und negativ fühlst, oder eine Exit-Strategie für die After-Work-Drinks am Donnerstagabend parat haben. Du wirst intuitiv wissen, ob dich eine Entscheidung deinem Ziel, nüchtern zu bleiben, näher bringt oder weiter davon entfernt.

Mit der Zeit wirst du zum Jedi des Energieflusses und verstehst, dass die Energie dorthin fließt, wo deine Aufmerksamkeit hingeht. Wenn du also nüchtern sein möchtest, konzentriere deine gesamte Energie darauf, nüchtern zu werden.

Du wirst es nicht bereuen.

KAPITEL 9:

FAZIT – ALLES WIRKT ZUSAMMEN

Dieses Buch gibt dir eine Menge Anregungen zum Nachdenken und Vertiefen. Niemand erwartet von dir, dass du jede Strategie umsetzt und dir jedes Detail sofort merkst. Das wäre überfordernd und ist unrealistisch. Dein Leben zu verändern ist ein Weg.

Sicherlich werden bestimmte Konzepte und Ideen bei dir mehr Anklang finden als andere. Also nimm diese auf und arbeite mit ihnen, während du dich auf das eine große Ziel konzentrierst: 24 Stunden am Stück nicht zu trinken.

Ich möchte dich ermutigen, dir diese Worte immer wieder vor Augen zu führen. Wahrscheinlich wirst du bei jedem Lesen andere „Heureka-Momente" erleben, vor allem, wenn du auf deinem eigenen Weg zur Nüchternheit vorankommst.

Um den Kreis zu schließen, lass uns noch einmal auf die Grundlage des Buches zurückkommen: 3 Nüchterne Schritte, die dir helfen, mit dem Trinken aufzuhören und nüchtern zu bleiben:

1. **Arbeite an deiner Selbstwahrnehmung.** Dann kannst du besser verstehen, *warum* du trinkst. Das ist wichtig, wenn du langfristig ein nüchternes Leben führen und nicht in einem Kreislauf aus Aufhören und Rückfall stecken bleiben möchtest.

2. **Ergreife positive Maßnahmen** – mit Hingabe und Konsequenz. So wirst du eher zu denjenigen gehören, die mit dem Trinken aufgehört haben, als zu denen, die nur darüber reden (und nichts dagegen tun).

3. **Der Aufbau der Intuition** wird mit der Zeit stattfinden, wenn du deine Selbstwahrnehmung verbesserst, die richtigen Maßnahmen ergreifst, um deinen Zielen näher zu kommen, und dich daran gewöhnst, die vielen Freuden zu erleben, die ein gesundes und nüchternes Leben mit sich bringt.

Die *3 Nüchternen Schritte* werden nicht immer der Reihe nach ablaufen. Manchmal bekommst du vielleicht ein intuitives Gefühl, dass etwas nicht stimmt, was dir erlaubt, den zweiten Schritt des Weges der Selbstwahrnehmung zu gehen.

Wie bereits zu Beginn beschrieben, ist es schwieriger, nüchtern zu bleiben, als mit dem Trinken aufzuhören. Deine Selbstwahrnehmung, dein positives Handeln und deine Intuition sind die Dinge, die du brauchst, um eine dauerhafte Veränderung zu bewirken – eine, bei der die Belohnungen und die positiven Kreisläufe immer wieder kommen.

Ich war der Trinker, der leidenschaftlich daran glaubte, dass Menschen, die sich nicht jeden Freitagabend betrinken, etwas „verpassen". Ich war der Trinker, der fest davon überzeugt war, dass ich mit der „Langeweile" des Nichttrinkens nie zurechtkommen würde. Ich war der Trinker, der mit sinnlosem Blödsinn wie „man kann nie jemandem vertrauen, der nicht trinkt" daherkam.

Heute wünschte ich mir nur, ich hätte die Realität der Nüchternheit früher entdeckt – ein authentisches, erfülltes Leben voller Abwechslung, Entdeckungen und dem unersetzbaren Gefühl, dass die Person, die ich im Spiegel sehe, jemand ist, den ich mag und respektiere.

Was in den Communitys für Nüchterne immer auffällt, ist die Freude und positive Energie, die dort herrscht. Nüchtern zu werden ist, als würdest du in ein Geheimnis eingeweiht. Es ist nichts, was die Menschen bedauern. Wenn es so wäre, würden die Leute feiern, wenn sie rückfällig werden. Das tun sie aber nicht.

Dieses Gefühl von beständiger Zufriedenheit und Positivität ist für alle erreichbar – auch für dich. Und mit dem unaufhaltsamen Anstieg derer, die "Sober Curious" sind, machen immer mehr Menschen diese Erfahrung. Alles, was es zu tun gilt, ist das Ziel zu verfolgen, 24 Stunden am Stück nicht zu trinken.

Worauf wartest du noch?

Mit nur einem Klick zur Bewertung!

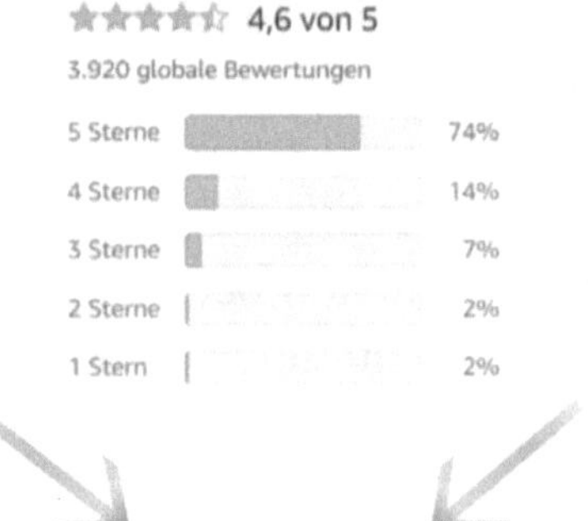

Kundenbewertung verfassen

Ich wäre dir sehr dankbar, wenn du dir nur 60 Sekunden Zeit nehmen würdest, um eine kurze Rezension auf Amazon zu schreiben, selbst wenn es nur ein paar Worte sind.

Hast du das Buch gelesen?

KENNST DU SCHON DEN INTERNATIONALEN BESTSELLER

Nüchtern auf einem alkoholisierten Planeten: Ohne Alkohol leben

- Die unerwartete Abkürzung zu Glück, Gesundheit und finanzieller Freiheit

ERHÄLTLICH BEI AMAZON

Join Our Community

If you need help in your sobriety journey, join our group of like-minded individuals who are all trying to live their best life, sober.

Scan the QR code below

Or

Join by visiting:

soberonadrunkplanet.com/ community

RESSOURCEN

Kenn dein Limit - eine Kampagne der BZgA:
https://www.kenn-dein-limit.de/

Selbsttest zum Umgang mit Alkohol:
https://www.kenn-dein-limit.de/alkohol-tests/alkohol-selbsttest/

Suchtvorbeugung und Hilfe für Suchtkranke:
https://www.blaues-kreuz.de/de/wege-aus-der-sucht/

Selbsthilfegruppen finden:
https://www.aktionswoche-alkohol.de/schwerpunktthema-2022-sucht-selbsthilfe/sucht-selbsthilfegruppe-finden/

Sober On A Drunk Planet – Podcast (Eng)

https://www.soberonadrunkplanet.com/podcasts/

Körperliche Entzugserscheinungen - mehr Informationen (Eng):

Drink Aware:

https://www.drinkaware.co.uk/facts/health-effects-of-alcohol/mental-health/alcohol-withdrawal-symptoms

NHS:

https://www.nhs.uk/conditions/alcohol-misuse/treatment/

Alcohol Change:

https://alcoholchange.org.uk/

Web MD:

https://www.webmd.com/mental-health/addiction/alcohol-withdrawal-symptoms-treatments#1

QUELLENVERZEICHNIS

[1] Mail Online. (2011, May 9). Pass the painkillers: The average Brit spends more than five YEARS of their life with a hangover. Retrieved from https://www.dailymail.co.uk/health/article-1385024/The-average-Brit-spends-5-YEARS-life-hangover.html

[2] DiLonardo, M. (2021, November 26). What Is Alcohol Withdrawal? Retrieved from https://www.webmd.com/mental-health/addiction/alcohol-withdrawal-symptoms-treatments#1

[3] Oxford Learner's Dictionaries. Self-awareness (noun). Retrieved from https://www.oxfordlearnersdictionaries.com/definition/english/self-awareness

[4] Duval, S & Wicklund, R. (1972). *A Theory of Objective Self Awareness*. Academic Press.

[5] Quote Investigator. Between Stimulus and Response There Is a Space. In That Space Is Our Power To Choose Our Response. Retrieved from https://quoteinvestigator.com/2018/02/18/response/

[6] Alcohol, Drugs and Development. (2012, October 21). Half the world's adults do not drink alcohol – what should the policy implications be? Retrieved from http://www.add-resources.org/half-the-worlds-adults-do-not-drink-alcohol-what-should-the-policy-implications-be.5325474-315773.html

[7] Mayo Clinic. Chronic stress puts your health at risk. Retrieved from https://www.mayoclinic.org/healthy-lifestyle/stress-management/in-depth/stress/art-20046037

[8] MedicalNewsToday. Cognitive dissonance: What to know. Retrieved from https://www.medicalnewstoday.com/articles/326738

[9] NHS. Drink Less. Retrieved from https://www.nhs.uk/better-health/drink-less/

[10] Vilhaue, J. (2020, September 27). How Your Thinking Creates Your Reality. Retrieved from https://www.psychologytoday.com/us/blog/living-forward/202009/how-your-thinking-creates-your-reality

[11] Quote Investigator. Faced With the Choice Between Changing One's Mind and Proving That There Is No Need To Do So, Almost Everyone Gets Busy On the Proof. Retrieved from https://quoteinvestigator.com/2018/05/17/change-view/

---

[12] Jarrett, C. (2016, September 9). Clues to your personality appeared before you could talk. Retrieved from https://www.bbc.com/future/article/20160907-clues-to-your-personality-appeared-before-you-could-talk

[13] Jarrett, C. (2016, September 9). Clues to your personality appeared before you could talk. Retrieved from https://www.bbc.com/future/article/20160907-clues-to-your-personality-appeared-before-you-could-talk

[14] Kaliszewski, M. (2022, September 9). The Link Between Child Abuse and Substance Abuse. Retrieved from https://americanaddictioncenters.org/blog/the-link-between-child-abuse-and-substance-abuse

[15] Tony Robbins. Reprogram your Mind. Retrieved from https://www.tonyrobbins.com/mind-meaning/how-to-reprogram-your-mind/

[16] Quote Investigator. Do One Thing Every Day That Scares You. Retrieved from https://quoteinvestigator.com/2013/08/09/scare/

[17] Cherry, K. (2022, February 18). What Is Neuroplasticity? Retrieved from https://www.verywellmind.com/what-is-brain-plasticity-2794886

[18] Taylor, A. (2020, January 27). The Right to Listen. Retrieved from https://www.newyorker.com/news/the-future-of-democracy/the-right-to-listen

19 Kerpen, D. 15 Quotes to Inspire You to Be a Better Listener. Retrieved from https://www.inc.com/dave-kerpen/15-quotes-to-inspire-you-to-become-a-better-listener.html

20 Nhat Hanh, T. (2010). *Reconciliation: Healing the Inner Child*. Parallax Press.

21 Kane, R. (2022, September 6). How Many People Meditate In The World? Retrieved from https://mindfulnessbox.com/how-many-people-meditate-in-the-world/

22 Schultz, J. (2020, July 24). 5 Differences Between Mindfulness and Meditation. Retrieved from https://positivepsychology.com/differences-between-mindfulness-meditation/

23 Solaris Pediatric Therapy. The Importance of the Vagal Nerve and the Nervous System. Retrieved from https://www.solarispediatrictherapy.com/blog/the-importance-of-the-vagal-nerve-and-the-nervous-system

24 Solanki, D & Lane, A. (2010). Relationships between Exercise as a Mood Regulation Strategy and Trait Emotional Intelligence. 1(4): 195–200. Retrieved from https://www.ncbi.nlm.nih.gov/pmc/articles/PMC3289183/

25 Daily Stoic. Marcus Aurelius Quotes. Retrieved from https://dailystoic.com/marcus-aurelius-quotes/

[26] UWA Online. (2019, May 17). Our Basic Emotions. Retrieved from https://online.uwa.edu/infographics/basic-emotions/

[27] He's Extraordinary. Improve Emotional Regulation In Just 7 Minutes Per Day. Retrieved from https://hes-extraordinary.com/improve-emotional-regulation-just-7-minutes-per-day

[28] Rees Anderson, A. (2015, April 7). Resentment Is Like Taking Poison And Waiting For The Other Person To Die. Retrieved from https://www.forbes.com/sites/amyanderson/2015/04/07/resentment-is-like-taking-poison-and-waiting-for-the-other-person-to-die/?sh=186a1172446c

[29] Keller, A. (2020, February 28). Alcohol and Dopamine. Retrieved from https://www.drugrehab.com/addiction/alcohol/alcoholism/alcohol-and-dopamine/

[30] Stewart, J. (2008). Psychological and neural mechanisms of relapse. 363(1507): 3147–3158. Retrieved from https://www.ncbi.nlm.nih.gov/pmc/articles/PMC2607321/

[31] Jedras, P, Jones A & Field M. (2013). The role of anticipation in drug addiction and reward. 2014(3): 1 -10. Retrieved from https://www.dovepress.com/the-role-of-anticipation-in-drug-addiction-and-reward-peer-reviewed-fulltext-article-NAN

[32] Pratt, M. (2022, February 17). The Science of Gratitude. Retrieved from https://www.mindful.org/the-science-of-gratitude/

[33] Emmons, R. A, & McCullough, M. E. (2003). Counting Blessings Versus Burdens: An Experimental Investigation of Gratitude and Subjective Well-Being in Daily Life. 84(2), 377. Retrieved from https://greatergood.berkeley.edu/pdfs/GratitudePDFs/6Emmons-BlessingsBurdens.pdf

[34] Recovery Nutrition. How Nutrition Can Support Becoming Alcohol-Free. Retrieved from https://www.recovery-nutrition.co.uk/blog/nutrition-to-support-being-alcohol-free

[35] WebMD. (2021, April 12). What to Know About VO2 Max. Retrieved from https://www.webmd.com/fitness-exercise/what-to-know-about-vo2-max

[36] Bird, S. & Hawley, J. (2017). Update on the effects of physical activity on insulin sensitivity in humans. 2(1): e000143. Retrieved from https://www.ncbi.nlm.nih.gov/pmc/articles/PMC5569266/

[37] Hep. (2016, December 19). Diet and Exercise Improve Liver and Kidney Health in Those With NASH. Retrieved from https://www.hepmag.com/article/diet-exercise-improve-liver-kidney-health-nash

38 WebMD. (2022, February 10). Diet and Lifestyle Tips to Reverse Fatty Liver Disease. Retrieved from https://www.webmd.com/hepatitis/fatty-liver-disease-diet

39 Healthline. (2019, January 30). How Aerobic Classes Can Make You a Better Problem Solver. Retrieved from https://www.healthline.com/health-news/want-to-be-a-better-problem-solver-try-doing-aerobics

40 Pacheco, D. (2022, May 6). Exercise and Sleep. Retrieved from https://www.sleepfoundation.org/physical-activity/exercise-and-sleep

41 Pacheco, D. (2022, September 19). Alcohol and Sleep. Retrieved from https://www.sleepfoundation.org/nutrition/alcohol-and-sleep

42 NHS. Benefits of Exercise. Retrieved from https://www.nhs.uk/live-well/exercise/exercise-health-benefits/

43 Singh, D. (2022, June 20). How yoga can help us heal from past trauma. Retrieved from https://www.indiatoday.in/news-analysis/story/how-yoga-can-help-us-heal-from-past-trauma-1964598-2022-06-20

[44] Looi, M. (2020, July 14). The human microbiome: Everything you need to know about the 39 trillion microbes that call our bodies home. Retrieved from https://www.sciencefocus.com/the-human-body/human-microbiome/

[45] WebMD. (2021, June 9). What Is Dysbiosis? Retrieved from https://www.webmd.com/digestive-disorders/what-is-dysbiosis

[46] Fu, J, Bonder, M, Cenit, M, Tigchelaar, E, Maatman, A, Dekens, J, Brandsma, E, Marczynska, J, Imhann, F, Weersma, R, Franke, L, Poon, T, Xavier, R, Gevers, D, Hofker, M, Wijmenga, C, & Zhernakova, A. (2015). The Gut Microbiome Contributes to a Substantial Proportion of the Variation in Blood Lipids. 117(9):817-24. Retrieved from https://pubmed.ncbi.nlm.nih.gov/26358192/

[47] Nutritious Life. How Gut Health Impacts Blood Sugar. Retrieved from https://nutritiouslife.com/eat-empowered/gut-health/gut-health-blood-sugar/

[48] Lucas, S, Rothwell, N, & Gibson, R. (2006). The role of inflammation in CNS injury and disease. 147(Suppl 1): S232–S240. Retrieved from https://www.ncbi.nlm.nih.gov/pmc/articles/PMC1760754/

[49] Healthline. Why the Gut Microbiome Is Crucial for Your Health. Retrieved from https://www.healthline.com/nutrition/gut-microbiome-and-health

[50] Carabotti, M, Scirocco, A, Maselli, M, & Severi, C. (2015). The gut-brain axis: interactions between enteric microbiota, central and enteric nervous systems. 28(2): 203–209. Retrieved from https://www.ncbi.nlm.nih.gov/pmc/articles/PMC4367209/

[51] NHS. Sugar: the facts. Retrieved from https://www.nhs.uk/live-well/eat-well/food-types/how-does-sugar-in-our-diet-affect-our-health

[52] FitRecovery. The Links Between Hypoglycaemia and Alcohol and How to Fix It. Retrieved from https://fitrecovery.com/alcoholism-and-hypoglycemia/

[53] Healthline. What Is Vibrational Energy? Retrieved from https://www.healthline.com/health/vibrational-energy

[54] Groth, A. (2012, July 14). You're The Average Of The Five People You Spend The Most Time With. Retrieved from https://www.businessinsider.com/jim-rohn-youre-the-average-of-the-five-people-you-spend-the-most-time-with-2012-7?r=US&IR=T

[55] Healthline. Grounding: Exploring Earthing Science and the Benefits Behind It. Retrieved from https://www.healthline.com/health/grounding